2017-2020 United Methodist Church Financial Records Handbook

for Treasurers, Financial Secretaries, and Other Church Officers

Contents

Prepared and edited by the General Council on Finance and Administration with the assistance of Mark F. Hagewood

Published by The United Methodist Publishing House. Copyright © 1976 by The United Methodist Publishing House. Revised edition copyright © 2018 by The United Methodist Publishing House. All rights reserved.
ISBN 9781501835711
Download Edition 9781501835728

Supplemental Digital Content

Purchasers of this book have online access to a PDF of the text and related documents. Go to www.UMOfficialResources.com/forms. To download the file, click on *2017–2020 United Methodist Church Financial Records Handbook Manual & Forms*. Double click on the file to open it or to save it to your desktop. Each time you open the file you will be prompted to enter the following password: **Aw38hW5t** (Please note that the password is case sensitive.)

Introduction

This handbook is designed to assist you in the work of extending Christ's love through the business of receiving, distributing, and reporting gifts given by God's people for the mission and ministry of the church. The handbook describes the basic financial records and procedures you need to receive, record, disburse, report, and manage the funds received by your church. It also provides instructions for good financial control and for using forms developed especially to assist United Methodist congregations.

The handbook is divided into three major sections: *The Work of the Counting Committee*, *The Work of the Financial Secretary*, and *The Work of the Treasurer*. Each section includes step-by-step directions to accomplish tasks that most churches tackle regularly including counting the offering, preparing and mailing reports of giving to donors, and preparing the periodic Treasurer's Report and other financial reports.

Much of this handbook is written for the financial secretary who keeps financial records on paper. At the same time, it is recognized that an increasing number of persons who keep such records have access to and want to use a computer to accomplish the task more efficiently.

If you do choose to use a computer for keeping the church's financial records, this handbook will still be of value to you. The kinds of records and reports needed, the procedures that should be followed in handling and accounting for church funds, the safeguards and controls that need to be in place to assure the proper use of funds entrusted to the church for the fulfillment of its ministry—none of that will change. You will have chosen a different set of tools to use in your stewardship of the resources God's people have made available for the task of proclaiming the gospel.

For churches that need a comprehensive record-keeping system or churches that plan to convert their financial records to a computer, the appendix "The General Ledger Approach—The Bridge to Financial Record Keeping on Computer" provides directions and reproducible masters for a general ledger system. Because many off-the-shelf software products are based on the use of a general ledger, setting up a manual general ledger is a helpful step toward converting your records to a PC or MAC.

A Biblical & Wesleyan Foundation

Records of the gifts given to God's glory and for God's service have been a part of our tradition from the beginning. The seventh chapter of the book of Numbers records, by tribe, what was contributed for the dedication of the altar of the tabernacle. The total, we are told, included twelve silver plates, twelve silver basins, and twelve golden dishes. The weight of each of these types of vessels is recorded, and there then follows an enumeration of animals given for burnt offerings, sin offerings, and peace offerings.

John Wesley admonished the early Methodists to "Earn all you can. Save all you can. Give all you can." And he encouraged them to make wise use of the gifts entrusted to them by God. As a church treasurer, financial secretary, or member of the counting com-mittee you are called to be a faithful and trusted steward —a person who helps your congregation care for, manage, and use the financial gifts contributed by the congregation for the service of God in your community and the world.

Basis in The Book of Discipline

The following paragraphs from Part VI, chapter one of *The Book of Discipline 2016* provide you with an overview of the purpose behind the careful organization and administration of the church and the disciplinary foundation for your task.

Excerpts are from *The Book of Discipline of The United Methodist Church 2016*, Copyright © 2016 by The United Methodist Publishing House. Used by permission.

Section VI. Organization and Administration

¶ 243. *Primary Tasks*—The local church shall be organized so that it can pursue its primary task and mission in the context of its own community—reaching out and receiving with joy all who will respond; encouraging people in their relationship with God and inviting them to commitment to God's love in Jesus Christ; providing opportunities for them to seek strengthening and growth in spiritual formation; and supporting them to live lovingly and justly in the power of the Holy Spirit as faithful disciples.

In carrying out its primary task, it shall be organized so that adequate provision is made for these basic responsibilities: (1) planning and implementing a program of nurture, outreach, and witness for persons and families within and without the congregation; (2) providing for effective pastoral and lay leadership; (3) providing for financial support, physical facilities, and the legal obligations of the church; (4) utilizing the appropriate relationships and resources of the district and annual conference; (5) providing for the proper creation, maintenance, and disposition of documentary record material of the local church; and (6) seeking inclusiveness in all aspects of its life.

The Church Council and the Church Budget

The Discipline *establishes the requirement for the church council, the composition of the council, and the responsibilities of this leadership group including:*

¶ 252.4c. Establish the budget on recommendation of the committee on finance and ensure adequate provision for the financial needs of the church.

¶ 252.4d. Recommend to the charge conference the salary and other remuneration of the pastor(s) and staff members after receiving recommendations from the committee on pastor-parish relations (staff-parish relations).

The Committee on Finance

In ¶ 258.4, the Discipline *establishes the requirement for the committee on finance, the composition of the committee, the responsibilities of the committee, the responsibilities of the finacial secretary, the treasurer, the counting committee as well as the requirement that the offices of treasurer and financial secretary must be filled with two individuals from different immediate families.*

¶ 258.4. [excerpt] All financial askings to be included in the annual budget of the local church shall be submitted to the committee on finance. The committee on finance shall compile annually a complete budget for the local church and submit it to the church council for review and adoption. The committee on finance shall be charged with responsibility for developing and implementing plans that will raise sufficient income to meet the budget adopted by the church council. It shall administer the funds received according to instructions from the church council.

The committee shall carry out the church council's directions in guiding the treasurer(s) and financial secretary.

a) The committee shall designate at least two persons not of the immediate family residing in the same household to count the offering. They shall work under the supervision of the financial secretary. A record of all funds received shall be given to the financial secretary and treasurer. Funds received shall be deposited promptly in accordance with the procedures established by the committee on finance. The financial secretary shall keep records of the contributions and payments.

b) The **church treasurer(s)** shall disburse all money contributed to causes represented in the local church budget, and such other funds and contributions as the church council may determine. The treasurer(s) shall remit each month to the conference treasurer all World Service and conference benevolence funds then on hand. Contributions to benevolence shall not be used for any cause other than that to which they have been given. The church treasurer shall make regular and detailed reports on funds received and expended to the committee on finance and the church council. (See Judicial Council Decisions 63, 320, 539.) The treasurer(s) shall be adequately bonded.

c) The committee on finance shall establish written financial policies to document the internal controls of the local church. The written financial policies should be reviewed for adequacy and effectiveness annually by the committee on finance and submitted as a report to the charge conference annually.

d) The committee shall make provision for an annual audit of the financial statements of the local church and all its organizations and accounts. The committee shall make a full and complete report to the annual charge conference. A local church audit is defined as an independent evaluation of the financial reports and records and the internal controls of the local church by a qualified person or persons.

The audit shall be conducted for the purpose of reasonably verifying the reliability of financial reporting, determining whether assets are being safeguarded, and determining compliance with local law, local church policies and procedures, and *The Book of Discipline*.

The audit may include: 1) a review of the cash and investment reconciliations; 2) interviews with the treasurer, financial secretary, pastor(s), finance committee chair, business manager, those who count offerings, church secretary, etc., with inquires regarding compliance with existing written financial policies and procedures; 3) a review of journal entries and authorized check signers for each checking and investment account; and 4) other procedures requested by the committee on finance.

The audit shall be performed by an audit committee composed of persons unrelated to the persons listed in (2) above or by an an independent certified public accountant (CPA), accounting firm, or equivalent.

e) The committee shall recommend to the church council proper depositories for the church's funds. Funds received shall be deposited promptly in the name of the local church.

f) Contributions designated for specific causes and objects shall be promptly forwarded according to the intent of the donor and shall not be used for any other purpose. (See Judicial Council Decision 976.)

g) After the budget of the local church has been approved, additional appropriations or changes in the budget must be approved by the church council.

h) The committee shall prepare annually a report to the church council of all designated funds that are separate from the current expense budget.

Basic Record Keeping

A good local church financial record system provides a historical record, reports that are clear and consistent, and a guide for planning and budgeting. Together with proper procedures for handling funds, it will also help to assure that funds are administered with integrity and in keeping with the plans and purposes for which they are given. Its proper use reinforces the donor's desire to support the ministry and mission of the church.

THE WORK OF THE COUNTING COMMITTEE

Receiving Funds—The Challenge of Accounting Control:

Accurate recording and reporting of gifts is dependent on a good receiving procedure and counting committee. Counters can be trained and rotated so that this goal is achieved in any size church. It is tempting for a church, large or small, to give the job to one person or to a husband and wife, but this is not good control, nor does it provide protection for the donors and counters against misunderstandings and charges of fraud.

Churches receive the majority of their funds through the Sunday or weekday offerings at the church, however some offerings are mailed or delivered by hand or submitted online. All situations require immediate control and careful handling.

It is not unusual to enter a church sanctuary or church school and see offering envelopes and cash in an unattended collection plate. This is not only poor accounting control, it is also poor stewardship to place temptation before persons who may struggle to deal with emotionally laden financial difficulties.

Checks and cash delivered to the church by individuals or groups pose similar control problems. How are such funds handled? Do they lie on a pastor's or secretary's desk or in a file until Sunday? Even if the church is closed during the week, where does the mail go? To the pastor? The treasurer? The financial secretary's home address? Many churches do not realize they have a problem until something goes wrong.

Controls for Receiving Funds

● **The membership of the counting committee.** Confirm that the counting committee is composed of at least two persons not of the same immediate family residing in the same household.
 —Also no matter what size church, for control and protection, neither the treasurer nor any other financial officer of the church should act as a member of the counting committee.

● **Secure offerings collected during services.** Designate a person to remove the offering from the altar and place it in the hands of a member of the counting committee as soon as the congregation begins to exit at the end of the service. IMPORTANT: *Never leave checks or cash unattended.*

● **Secure offerings made during class meetings.** Have each class leader place the class offering in the hands of a designated member of the counting committee.

● **Secure offerings that are mailed, delivered to the church, or made online. Select the option that fits your situation:**
 —Have such offerings mailed to a post office box.
 —Have offerings mailed to a bank where you have made arrangements to have it held for the counters.
 —Establish one address to which all such offerings should be mailed or delivered, and advise the congregation of this address periodically perhaps in the weekly bulletin or newsletter.
 —Designate two persons to count, record, and deposit interim receipts as received.
 —Create a record of such gifts to place in the offering plate for dedication during the next regular worship service.
 —Receive reports for any gifts that are made online through EFT (electronic fund transfer), debit card, or credit card.

● **Establish how offerings are to be secured until counting.**
 —Designate a member of the counting committee to either take the offering immediately to the regularly

designated place for counting, or
 —If counting is done at a later time, designate a committee member to immediately place the offering in a lockable bag or other secure receptacle and deliver it to a bank night depository. The bag may then be claimed later by the designated counting committee member and taken to an appropriate location for counting.

● **Establish a secure location for counting.** Select a secure room for counting that is removed from easy line of sight of passersby and away from the regular foot traffic patterns of persons who are not part of the counting committee.

● **Determine if you need extra security.** In some circumstances—especially if your offerings include large amounts of cash—arrange to count your offering at the bank. Have several members of the congregation deliver your receipts to the bank or arrange for a police escort.

● **Provide the space and tools your counters need to do good work.** Provide adequate space, clear table surfaces, scratch pads, paper clips, coin and currency wrappers, a supply of forms, an adding machine or calculator with a tape, and any other supplies the counters need. Also provide the counters with:
 —list of regular donors and their pledges
 —list of budgeted and unbudgeted receipts a counter might receive.
These arrangements will speed the process and improve the accuracy.

COUNTER'S TALLY SHEET

	Checks	Currency	Coin	TOTAL
Loose Plate Offering	_____	_____	_____	_____
Special-fund Offerings	_____	_____	_____	_____
Regular/Pledge Offerings	_____	_____	_____	_____
Church School Offering	_____	_____	_____	_____
Miscellaneous receipts	_____	_____	_____	_____

_____   _____
Counter Signature   Counter Signature

Counting the Offering

● **Establish a sound procedure for counting and follow it regularly.** Counters will develop a feel for the process and for who does what best and in what sequence. A sound procedure will contain these steps, not necessarily in this exact sequence:

(1) **Sort the plate contents into:**
—loose plate offering (currency and coins)
—special-fund offering envelopes
—regular pledge/tithe offering envelopes
—miscellaneous envelopes and loose checks

(2) **Count the loose plate offerings (currency and coins) twice to confirm the total.** On a tally sheet such as the one illustrated on the next page, record the subtotals for each deposit category (currency, coins) and the total.

(3) **Identify and group together the loose checks received without envelopes that are clearly pledges or identifiable offerings.**
—NOTE: Make sure that counters have access to the names of the pledgers.
—Use a REMITTANCE ADVICE FORM (such as the one shown below) to make a record of each check for the financial secretary. Enter the donor's name(s), address, amount of the check, purpose (pledge, tithe, special fund, etc.), date, and counter's name. You may design your own REMITTANCE ADVICE FORM or use a supply of the previous year's unused offering envelopes with the old identity numbers inked out.

REMITTANCE ADVICE FORM

Advice to the Financial Secretary of funds received from:

Name _____

Address _____

_____

Amount _____ Purpose(s) _____

Date _____ Counter _____

—Sort the loose checks and their REMITTANCE ADVICE FORMS into the appropriate group of offerings: special-funds or pledge/tithe.

—NOTE: A listing of the loose checks may work for your situation, but remember that separate REMITTANCE ADVICE FORMS or offering envelopes help the counters sort the offerings and allow the financial secretary to arrange the offerings in sequence to prepare the monthly or quarterly reports of giving.

(4) **Open the special-fund offering envelopes and determine if the amount enclosed matches the amount written on the envelope.** Circle the amount the donor has indicated on the envelope to show it agrees with what was inside, or, if the donor has not indicated the amount, write it on the envelope in the space provided and initial. If the contents do not agree with the donor's indications on the envelope, do not circle. Write in the amount actually received in a place on the envelope where the financial secretary will see it *first* (colored ink is good) and initial. <u>Do not erase or cross out the donor's figure.</u>

If needed, add the donor's identity to the envelope. Where an envelope number is used, the giver's name need not be present, but it is a good cross-check. Where the name is not present, you may be able to transcribe it from an enclosed check. If there is no identity or number on a cash gift provided in an offering envelope, indicate this by writing "cash" or the letter "C" on the envelope.

(5) **Count the checks, currency, and coin that you have removed from the special-fund offering envelopes (plus the loose checks you have identified as special-fund offerings).** Run subtotals on each deposit category (checks, currency, coins) and the total for all the special offering money. Record the subtotals and the total on your tally sheet.

(6) **To cross-check yourself, add the amounts written on the special-fund offering envelopes and determine if the total matches your count of the money.** If your total for the envelopes does not match your total for the money, recheck your count of the checks, currency, and coin. Next, think about some other obvious error, such as transposition of figures or a loose check without a REMITTANCE ADVICE FORM. Check the adding machine tape to confirm that amounts written on the envelopes were keyed correctly. These steps should disclose the difference. If not, make the proper notations on your adding machine tapes for the envelopes and for the money. Hold the balanced tapes and money.

(7) **Open the regular pledge offering envelopes and determine if the amount enclosed matches the amount written on the envelope.** Follow the same procedure you used for checking the special-fund offerings: Circle the amount the donor has indicated on the envelope to show it agrees with what was inside, or, if the donor has not indicated the amount, write it on the envelope in the space provided and initial. If the contents do not agree with the donor's indications on the envelope, <u>do not circle</u>. Write in the amount actually received in a place on the envelope where the financial secretary will see it *first* (colored ink is good) and initial. <u>Do not erase or cross out the donor's figure.</u>

(8) **Count the checks, currency, and coin that you have removed from the regular pledge offering envelopes (plus the loose checks that you have identified as regular offerings).** Run subtotals on each deposit category (checks, currency, coins) and then a total for all the regular pledge offering money. Record the subtotals and the total on your tally sheet.

(9) **To cross-check yourself, add the amounts written on the regular offering envelopes and Remittance Advice Forms and determine if the total matches your count of the money.** If your total for the envelopes does not match your total for the money, recheck your count of the checks, currency, and coin. Next, think about some other obvious error, such as transposition of figures or a loose check without a REMITTANCE ADVICE FORM. Check the adding machine tape to confirm that amounts written on the envelopes were keyed correctly. These steps should disclose the difference. If not, make the proper notations on your adding machine tapes for the envelopes and for the money. Hold the balanced tapes and money.

No. _____

CASH RECEIPTS VOUCHER

Date_____

To: **Treasurer**   **Financial Secretary**   **Pastor**

Deposited to _____ Account: $ _____
Deposited to _____ Account: $ _____
Deposited to _____ Account: $ _____

Summary of Receipts
Annual Operating Budget & Benevolences Giving Funding Sources:

	Received From Pledgers	Received From Non-Pledgers/Identified Givers	Received From Unidentified Givers	Totals
Budget.				
Benevolences				
Other:				
_____				
_____				
_____				

Other Funding Sources:
Interest & Dividend . . . . _____
Sale of Church Assets . . . . _____
Builiding Use Fees, Contributions, & Rentals . . . . _____
Fundraisers/Other:

_____ . . . . _____
_____ . . . . _____

Funding Sources for Capital and Other Special Projects:
Capital Campaigns . . . . _____
Memorial/Endowment Bequests . . . . _____
Special Sundays, Advance Specials, and Other Forms of Directed Benevolent Giving . . . . _____
Other Sources and Projects:

_____ . . . . _____
_____ . . . . _____

Funding Sources from District(s), Annual Conference(s), Jurisdictional Conference(s), General Church and/or other institutional sources outside the local Church
Equitable Compensation Funds received by Church or Pastor . . . . _____
Advance Special or Apportioned Funds Received by Church . . . . _____
Other:

_____ . . . . _____
_____ . . . . _____

Totals . . . . _____

Date _____

_____

_____

_____

Counters Signatures

No. 10

CASH RECEIPTS VOUCHER

Date _3/10/11_

| To: | Treasurer | Financial Secretary | Pastor |

Deposited to _Checking_   Account: $ _590.00_
Deposited to _____ Account: $ _____
Deposited to _____ Account: $ _____

Summary of Receipts
Annual Operating Budget & Benevolences Giving Funding Sources:

	Received From Pledgers #321	Received From Non-Pledgers/Identified Givers #325	Received From Unidentified Givers #331	Totals
Budget	250.00	75.00	15.00	340.00
Benevolences				
Other:				
_____				
_____				
_____				

Other Funding Sources:
Interest & Dividend .... _____
Sale of Church Assets .... _____
Builiding Use Fees, Contributions, & Rentals #345 .... 225.00
Fundraisers/Other:
_____ .... _____
_____ .... _____

Funding Sources for Capital and Other Special Projects:
Capital Campaigns .... _____
Memorial/Endowment Bequests #365 .... 25.00
Special Sundays, Advance Speicials, and Other Forms of Directed Benevolent Giving .... _____
Other Sources and Projects:
_____ .... _____
_____ .... _____

Funding Sources from District(s), Annual Conference(s), Jurisdictional Conference(s),
General Church and/or other institutional sources outside the local Church
Equitable Compensation Funds received by Church or Pastor .... _____
Advance Special or Apportioned Funds Received by Church .... _____
Other:
_____ .... _____
_____ .... _____

Totals 590.00

Date _3/10/11_

Mary M. Mitchell
John Smith
Counter Signatures

On the example above, the treasurer has indicated the account number for each item.

Preparing the Cash Receipts Voucher

- **Photocopy a supply of the Cash Receipts Voucher form** provided on the next page or create a customized form for your church that includes your standard budgeted and unbudgeted items.

- **Secure from the treasurer or your committee on finance a list of the miscellaneous budgeted and unbudgeted receipts** that you might be expected to receive each Sunday.

- **Count all miscellaneous funds received and record them on the Cash Receipts Voucher in the appropriate sections.** Budgeted items might include items such as rentals, sales, and budgeted special-fund offerings. Unbudgeted items might include gifts or some unscheduled special offering. —NOTE: The list of expected receipts provided by the treasurer or committee on finance should be helpful in identifying the correct category for each receipt. —Also, if you receive a large number of miscellaneous receipts involving several categories, make an adding machine tape, transcribe the subtotals of each category to the CASH RECEIPTS VOUCHER, and balance against the actual count of the money.

- **Enter the receipts for the Annual Operating Budget & Benevolences Giving Fund Sources.** Enter the totals for Budget, Benevolences, and other causes in the appropriate columns depending on whether the contributor is a pledger or non-pledger but identified giver. If pledges are made to a unified budget, then use either the BUDGET line or the blank line to record the regular pledge offerings.

- **Enter the loose currency/coin offerings.** Enter the totals under Received Unidentified Givers column.

- **Enter the loose Church School Offerings.** Enter the totals on the lines for Other Funding Sources. If your church does not maintain the CHURCH SCHOOL OFFERING and the loose plate offering separately, then enter the combined total on the UNIDENTIFIED GIVERS column.

- **Amount received for Special Sundays, General Advance Specials, World Service Specials, and other forms of directed benevolent (charitable) giving.** Enter the total received for benevolent causes including Special Sunday offerings, General Advance and World Service special gifts, and other forms of designated donations given by individuals and forwarded by the local church.

- **Enter the totals for other receipts by category** .

- **Use the adding machine (or calculator with a tape) to total each column.** Crossfoot total columns 1, 2, and 3 to column 4. (That is, confirm that the totals of columns 1, 2, and 3 equal column 4.) If they do not balance, check for adding and transcription errors and correct until totals crossfoot.
- **Use your adding machine or calculator to run a tape of the grand total of checks, currency, and coin**; and balance the total of all money to the total in column 4.

Preparing the Bank Deposit and Completing the Cash Receipts Voucher

- **Fill out your bank deposit slip and balance it to the CASH RECEIPTS VOUCHER.** Differences between your bank deposit slip total and the CASH RECEIPTS VOUCHER total are usually due to errors in transcription or in picking up a subtotal in one of the various cash categories. —NOTE: It is easier (and provides better control in most cases) to run subtotal tapes on cash in each category, using the tally sheet or marked adding-machine tapes. Experience may show that on small deposits this is not necessary.

- **Complete the Cash Receipts Voucher.** Fill in the date *counted*, the sequential number, and the account number to which each deposit is to be made.

- **Sign the Cash Receipts Voucher.** At least two persons should sign in the space provided. It is not necessary that all sign when larger teams of counters are used, but having everyone sign does provide a good record.

- **Make four photocopies of the Cash Receipts Voucher.** —**Original copy to treasurer:** Distribute the original copy of the CASH RECEIPTS VOUCHER along with a copy of the deposit slip and any adding machine deposit tapes to the **treasurer.** You may send it to the treasurer by mail or delivery, or you may simply place it in a designated location within the church office.

—**Copy to financial secretary**: Distribute a copy of the CASH RECEIPTS VOUCHER, proof tape of CASH RECEIPTS VOUCHER, tapes of contributions, and all offering envelopes and REMITTANCE ADVICE FORMS to the financial secretary as prearranged.

—**Copy to the pastor**: Distribute a copy of the CASH RECEIPTS VOUCHER to the pastor or the church secretary as prearranged.

—**Copy to the auditor**: Mail a copy of the CASH RECEIPTS VOUCHER and the deposit slip directly from the counting committee to the auditor designated by the church at an address outside of the church.

● **Prepare the bank deposit pouch.** Place the strapped and wrapped checks, currency, coin, and two copies of the deposit slip in a bank deposit pouch.

—NOTE: Arrange for the bank to return a receipted deposit slip to the treasurer.

● **Deposit the bank deposit pouch** *at once* **in a night depository.**

—NOTE: When more than one treasurer or bank account is involved, prepare separate deposits and reports for each.

THE WORK OF THE FINANCIAL SECRETARY

Recording and Reporting Offerings

Your job as the financial secretary entails keeping an accurate record of people's pledges and gifts without pressing them for a payment. There is, however, a very definite responsibility to keep the givers informed of the status of their giving and about the difference it makes in the ministry and mission of their church in the community and beyond.

The church council will establish the policies on how to keep givers informed and encouraged. Such policies may specify the format for the REPORT OF GIVING form as well as how often they should be prepared and distributed—quarterly, monthly, or on some other schedule.

The IRS and Charitable Contributions

The Internal Revenue Service (IRS) has set specific requirements for substantiating contributions that each financial secretary and church treasurer must learn and follow. Keep a careful record of all contributions and give each donor a written acknowledgement of all contributions over $250. The written acknowledgements must contain a statement similar to this: *No goods or services were provided to you by the church in connection with any contribution or their value consisted entirely of intangible religious benefits.* Follow these rules and make yourself aware of other IRS requirements for non-cash gifts of property and for donations for which a material benefit is provided such as a fund-raising dinner.

For more information contact your annual conference treasurer, access the IRS at www.irs.gov, or review the "GCFA Tax Packet" at www.gcfa.org.

Commitment Cards

The commitment card developed for United Methodist churches shown on the next page should work well for many congregations. It is designed to provide:

—A place for each donor to record their commitment during the annual church-funding campaign

—An encouragement to percentage giving

—A perforated tear-off control stub for accountability during the solicitation.

There are many types of cards in use. You may receive a card or a transcript of each donor's pledge as determined by the finance committee. You will enter each donor's pledge amounts on the REPORT OF GIVING form that you prepare for each donor. ("Donor," as used here, means each individual or giving unit who gives to the church.)

Quarterly Report of Giving

The QUARTERLY REPORT OF GIVING form shown on page 14 provides four reports to the donors and a permanent record of giving for the church archives. The secretary may compose letters or short reports for special mailings requested by the committee on finance at other points in the year.

Initiate the QUARTERLY REPORT OF GIVING forms for each donor in the church annually.

Card No._____

Name _____

Address _____

_____ **Phone** _____

A COMMITMENT TO THE CHURCH

In grateful recognition that all my (our) time, treasure(s), and ability(ies) come from God, I(we) gladly join with others in the support of Christ's church.

Per Week ❑   Per Month ❑   or _____ ❑

$_____for local ministries, including worship, education, pastoral service, church care and upkeep, and the world outreach of the church.

_____   _____
Signature   Date

_____   _____
Signature   Date

This commitment may be adjusted by presenting your request to the church office.

Card No. _____

Team Leader _____

Team Number _____

This card taken by:

Name _____

and

Name _____

Leave this stub with your Team Leader.

(See reverse side)

This is a control stub to be kept by the chairperson of the local church-funding program. This ensures proper accountability of cards at all times.

INCOME AND CHURCH SUPPORT

The table printed below is intended to aid you in estimating your weekly gifts to the church, based on the incomes listed in the first column. Tithing (10%) has been the traditional standard of giving in the church.

Weekly Income	Weekly Tithe (10%)	5%	7%	9%	11%	13%	15%	20%
50	5.00	2.50	3.50	4.50	5.50	6.50	7.50	10.00
100	10.00	5.00	7.00	9.00	11.00	13.00	15.00	20.00
200	20.00	10.00	14.00	18.00	22.00	26.00	30.00	40.00
300	30.00	15.00	21.00	27.00	33.00	39.00	45.00	60.00
400	40.00	20.00	28.00	36.00	44.00	52.00	60.00	80.00
500	50.00	25.00	35.00	45.00	55.00	65.00	75.00	100.00
750	75.00	37.50	52.50	67.50	82.50	97.50	112.50	150.00
1000	100.00	50.00	70.00	90.00	110.00	130.00	150.00	200.00
1500	150.00	75.00	105.00	135.00	165.00	195.00	225.00	300.00
2000	200.00	100.00	140.00	180.00	220.00	260.00	300.00	400.00
3000	300.00	150.00	210.00	270.00	330.00	390.00	450.00	600.00
5000	500.00	250.00	350.00	450.00	550.00	650.00	750.00	1000.00

Prepared and Edited by the General Council on Finance and Administration
0-687-43047X   The United Methodist Publishing House   Printed in U.S.A. 2001

This commitment card designed for The United Methodist Church is available from Cokesbury. Product number 9780687430475.

QUARTERLY REPORT OF GIVING

Env. No. _____

COL. 1	CURRENT EXPENSES OR UNIFIED BUDGET	
COL. 2	BENEVO-LENCES OR	
COL. 3	BUILDING FUND OR	

COMMITMENT:

☐ Weekly   ☐ Monthly

☐ _____

WE ACKNOWLEDGE WITH APPRECIATION YOUR GIFT AS RECORDED. REGULAR CONTRIBUTIONS ENABLE US TO MEET OUR FINANCIAL OBLIGATIONS PROMPTLY. CONTACT THE FINANCIAL OFFICER IF YOU HAVE QUESTIONS REGARDING THIS REPORT. PURSUANT TO INTERNAL REVENUE CODE REQUIREMENTS FOR SUBSTANTIATION OF CHARITABLE CONTRIBUTIONS, NO GOODS OR SERVICES WERE PROVIDED IN RETURN FOR THE ABOVE CONTRIBUTIONS.

Church:

Pursuant to Internal Revenue Code requirements for substantiation of charitable contributions, no goods or services were provided in return for the above contributions.

SUN	1st QUARTER			2nd QUARTER			3rd QUARTER			4th QUARTER		
	1	2	3	1	2	3	1	2	3	1	2	3
1												
2												
3												
4												
5												
6												
7												
8												
9												
10												
11												
12												
13												
14												
TOT. QTLY.												
PLEG. TO DATE												
PAID TO DATE												
BAL. TO DATE												

DESIGNATED GIFTS AND SPECIAL OFFERINGS

DATE	PURPOSE	AMOUNT	DATE	PURPOSE	AMOUNT
		TOTAL SPECIAL GIFTS FOR YEAR		
		TOTAL FOR YEAR BUDGET AND SPEC. GIFTS		

| DETACH BEFORE INITIALING | DATE | | OFFICERS INITIALS |

PLEASE RETAIN FOR INCOME TAX REFERENCE

The Quarterly Report of Giving designed for The United Methodist Church is available from Cokesbury. Product number 0687430496.

Matching window envelope is number 068743050X.

Initiating the Quarterly Report of Giving

- Obtain a list of the names and addresses for all individuals and families who are potential donors within the church constituency.

- Enter each name and mailing address along with the assigned envelope number on the QUARTERLY REPORT OF GIVING form.
  —NOTE: Some donors may not be issued offering envelopes, but you should still provide them with a report.

- Arrange the forms in numerical order.

- Date and initial each QUARTERLY REPORT OF GIVING form as you complete it.

- Transcribe the appropriate data from each donor's commitment card to the commitment section of the QUARTERLY REPORT OF GIVING form.
  —NOTE: The completed commitment section on the QUARTERLY REPORT OF GIVING form gives the financial secretary and the donor a record of the pledged amounts.
  —Spaces have been provided for fund names other than those shown.
  —Note the key for columns 1, 2, and 3 at the top of the QUARTERLY REPORT OF GIVING form. If your church has a totally unified budget system, use the appropriate spaces in column 1. If the budgeting and pledging include separate funds such as "current expenses" and "building" designations, then use columns 1, 3, and so on.

To Do Weekly:
Post Weekly Giving Information to Reports

- By Monday of each week obtain the following documents from the counting committee:
  —the CASH RECEIPTS VOUCHER,
  —the proof tape of the CASH RECEIPTS VOUCHER,
  —tapes of contributions, and
  —all offering envelopes and REMITTANCE ADVICE FORMS

- Confirm that records are in balance and complete. Compare the totals on the CASH RECEIPTS VOUCHER with the tape totals. Look for any special notations.

- To facilitate posting, sort the offering envelopes and REMITTANCE ADVICE FORMS into the same sequence as the QUARTERLY REPORT OF GIVING forms.
  —NOTE: The center of the report form provides space for you to enter the donor's offerings for each Sunday in a given quarter. The form also includes space to enter accumulated totals for the quarter and the year to date.
  —Use the lower section of the report to record designated and special giving that is not part of pledge or regular giving. These are totaled at the end of the year.

- Working from the offering envelopes and the REMITTANCE ADVICE FORMS, post each donor's offerings to their QUARTERLY REPORT OF GIVING form.

- Enter the DESIGNATED GIFTS AND SPECIAL OFFERINGS by date, purpose, and amount as received.

- When you have completed all the posting, run a tape of the entries and cross-check the total to column 1 on the CASH RECEIPTS VOUCHER (*credits to contributor's report of giving*).
  —IMPORTANT: These must agree. If they do not, follow the exception procedure developed and adopted by the committee on finance and the church council. A quick check with the counters or the treasurer will often resolve any discrepancy. Contact the contributor if you are unable to clear up the matter. If it involves a question of an accurate recording, however, remember to *be extremely tactful when you communicate with donors*. Money is a sensitive issue.

Keeping Records for Audits and Taxes

In addition to facilitating an internal audit, a financial secretary may be called upon to furnish records for income tax auditing several years after the gifts were made. While the giving report record will usually suffice, the source document (offering envelope) will help support the accuracy of that record in case of dispute. Tax and other audits have sometimes revealed substantial differences in the donor's and church's records of giving. Adequate controls to protect all persons involved are very important and will help avoid personal grievances and financial loss to the church and to the members.

To Do Quarterly:
Prepare and Mail the Quarterly Reports of Giving

- After posting the offerings for the last Sunday in the quarter, add the totals for the quarter.

- Calculate each donor's PLEDGE TO DATE and enter the amount in the designated space. If there is no pledge, make no entry.

- Calculate and enter the PAID TO DATE total. In the first quarter it will equal the total for the quarter. In subsequent quarters, it will equal the previous quarters' PAID TO DATE totals, plus the total for the current quarter.

- The BALANCE TO DATE entry will equal the difference between PLEDGE TO DATE and PAID TO DATE. If there is no PLEDGE TO DATE, make no BALANCE TO DATE entry.

- IMPORTANT: Never use minus signs or different colors to code the BALANCE TO DATE. Such signals may cause a donor to see red even if the color of ink is blue!

- If the PAID TO DATE is less than the PLEDGE TO DATE, enter the difference. If the PAID TO DATE is the same as PLEDGE TO DATE, indicate a zero balance. If the PAID TO DATE is more than the PLEDGE TO DATE, make no balance entry.

- Remove the top page from the QUARTERLY REPORT OF GIVING each quarter. Add the date, your initials, and mail it to the donor.

To Do Annually:

- You have entered the DESIGNATED GIFTS AND SPECIAL OFFERINGS by date, purpose, and amount as received each week. At the end of the year, total these amounts in the TOTAL SPECIAL GIFTS FOR YEAR space.

- Add the TOTAL SPECIAL GIFTS FOR YEAR to the total for the regular giving and enter that total in the TOTAL FOR YEAR, BUDGET AND SPECIAL GIFTS space.

- Remember, the church should *at least* give a statement to each donor annually (by January 31st).

Stuffing Envelopes and Mailing the Reports

- Work out the details of the mailing to suit the needs and help available in your church.

- Clear with the committee on finance and the church office a schedule for mailing the reports.

- NOTE: QUARTERLY REPORT OF GIVING forms must be mailed **first class** because each contains different data, however, if generated by a computer, these documents may be bulk mailed as they are not bills.

- **Make your quarterly or monthly mailings a positive opportunity to communicate with church members.** Many churches include a greeting from the pastor, announcements, or other helpful items in the mailing for the minimum first-class rate. Combining mailings in this way helps save on postage and helps remove any unintentional negative pressure.

- Enlist a crew of volunteers for stuffing and mailing. Emphasize confidentiality. Donors' giving records are personal and private.

- Provide the volunteers with supplies they need:
  —Stamped or metered mailing envelopes
  —QUARTERLY REPORT OF GIVING sheets to be mailed
  —Postage-paid reply envelopes (if needed)
  —Leaflets or letters to be mailed with the reports

- If window envelopes are used, fold the QUARTERLY REPORT OF GIVING sheet so that the address is visible in the window. (Small marks on the form show where to fold it.)

- If window envelopes are not used, then address the envelopes and put them in the same order as the reports. IMPORTANT: Ask volunteers to confirm that the envelope and the report match by name and number.

- And finally—be available to answer questions about the report. Enclose with the mailing a note providing a convenient telephone number and suggest hours for inquiry to help donors contact you.

THE WORK OF THE TREASURER

Recording Receipts, Disbursing Funds, and Reporting

The receipt and disbursement of money demand very careful attention to detail and accuracy. People are particularly sensitive to funds with which they have a personal identification.

Contributions to the church represent an extension of people's time, talent, and energy. Church treasurers have a very special stewardship role in processing these funds.

This section covers the entry, summarization, and reporting of financial transactions by the treasurer.

The New Church Treasurer— Getting Started

A treasurer succeeding to the job should insist upon an audit of the beginning balance and the records to support it by the official church auditor or someone appointed for this specific purpose. The incoming treasurer can and should go over the previous year's records with the outgoing treasurer to get started, but the audit should still take place. This helps prevent misunderstandings that later may be damaging to one or all parties. It catches any discrepancies while the circumstances are current and adjustments can be easily accomplished.

Chart of Accounts

A CHART OF ACCOUNTS is basic to financial record keeping. Stated simply, it is a list of the accounts to which financial transactions will be posted as they occur. Typically, a CHART OF ACCOUNTS includes a unique code number for each account. As transactions are recorded, the code or account number serves as a shorthand reference, enabling the person who keeps the records and those who use them to identify similar transactions quickly.

The CHART OF ACCOUNTS will vary widely in complexity from church to church. The church treasurer will usually decide on the number and types of accounts needed, based on the following considerations:

- The volume and complexity of the church's anticipated financial transactions.

- The amount of detail needed for reports to the committee on finance, the church council or administrative council/board, and the annual conference.

- The judgment of the treasurer, in consultation with the pastor and other church officers, about the kinds of financial information that will be most helpful as the church plans for the fulfillment of its missional goals.

The sample CHART OF ACCOUNTS on the next page includes accounts that will enable the treasurer to keep track of the current value of all of the church's assets (equipment, furnishings, and property of all kinds, as well as cash) and its liabilities as they are incurred. It thereby facilitates the preparation of a BALANCE SHEET. (For more on accounting procedures related to assets, liabilities, STATEMENT OF FINANCIAL STATEMENT(s), and STATEMENT OF ACTIVITIES, see the appendix: "The General Ledger Approach.") You may shorten, expand, or adapt the suggested CHART OF ACCOUNTS to meet the needs of your particular church.

Use the sample CHART OF ACCOUNTS as a guide to create your own CHART OF ACCOUNTS or to update the CHART OF ACCOUNTS used by the previous treasurer. Your church may not have as many accounts as we show in the sample or it may have more; but the accounts it has should be comparable to this list. If they are not, consider revising your CHART OF ACCOUNTS. The account classifications in the sample are designed to feed easily into the year-end LOCAL CHURCH REPORT TO THE ANNUAL CONFERENCE, TABLE II and TABLE III.

Beginning Your Record Keeping

- Verify the opening cash balance using the bank statement and the cash balance at the end of the period from the last TREASURER'S REPORT. Then start with the first CASH RECEIPTS VOUCHER and the CASH RECEIPTS JOURNAL.

Cash Receipts Vouchers and Deposit Slips

- Arrange with the counting committee to have them send you a copy of the CASH RECEIPTS VOUCHER each week, along with a copy of the deposit slip and a tape of the totals.

CHART OF ACCOUNTS

Code #	Account Title
ASSETS	
120	Petty cash
121	Checking Account
122	Savings Account
123	Investments
125	Receivables
150	Equipment
151	Vehicles
152	Parsonage
154	Church
155	Land

LIABILITIES AND FUNDS

LIABILITIES

Code #	Account Title
211	Payables
212	Social Security Tax Withholding
213	Federal Income Tax Withholding
214	State Income Tax Withholding
215	Local Income Tax Withholding
216	Group Insurance Withholding
217	Other Withholding
218	Employee/Pastor Withholding Reserves/Pension Withholding
219	Medicare Tax Withholding
220	Notes Payable
221	Long-Term Debt

FUNDS

Code #	Account Title
250	Designated Benevolences
251-289	Designated & Special Funds
290	General Fund

INCOME

RECEIPTS FOR ANNUAL OPERATING BUDGET & BENEVOLENCE GIVING SOURCES

Code #	Account Title
321	Received Through Pledges
325	Received from Non-pledging, yet Identified Givers
331	Received from Unidentified Givers
335	Received from Interest and Dividends
341	Received from Sale of Church Assets
345	Received through Building Use Fees, Contributions, Rentals
351	Received through Fundraisers and Other Sources

TOTAL ANNUAL OPERATING BUDGET & BENEVOLENCE RECEIPTS

RECEIPTS FOR CAPITAL AND OTHER SPECIAL PROJECTS

Code #	Account Title
361	Capital Campaigns
365	Memorial/Endowment Bequests
371	Human Relations Day
372	One Great Hour of Sharing
373	Peace with Justice Sunday
374	Native American Ministries Sunday
375	World Communion
376	U.M. Student Day
391	Other Sources and Projects

TOTAL CAPITAL AND OTHER SPECIAL PROJECTS RECEIPTS

RECEIPTS FROM DISTRICT(S), ANNUAL CONFERENCE(S), JURISDICTIONAL CONFERENCE(S), GENERAL CHURCH AND/OR OTHER INSTITUTIONAL SOURCES OUTSIDE THE LOCAL CHURCH

Code #	Account Title
381	Equitable Compensation Funds Received by Church or Pastor
385	Advance Special or Apportioned Funds Received by Church

TOTAL DISTRICT(S), ANNUAL CONFERENCE(S), JURISDICTIONAL CONFERENCE(S), GENERAL CHURCH AND/OR OTHER INSTITUTIONAL SOURCES OUTSIDE THE LOCAL CHURCH RECEIPTS

EXPENSES

BENEVOLENCES

Code #	Account Title
401	World Service
402	Conference Benevolences
403	Ministerial Education Fund
404	Black College Fund
405	Africa University Fund
406	General Advance Specials
407	World Service Special Gifts
408	Youth Service Fund
409	Human Relations Day
410	One Great Hour of Sharing
411	Peace With Justice Sunday
412	Native American Ministries Sunday
413	World Communion
414	U.M. Student Day
415	Christian Education Sunday
416	Golden Cross Sunday
417	Rural Life Sunday
418	Disability Awareness Sunday
419	Conference Advance Specials
420	Other Conference Appeals
421	Higher Education
422	Health & Welfare Agencies
423	Other Benevolences Sent to Conference
424	Other Benevolences Paid Direct

CONNECTIONAL ADMINISTRATION FUNDS

Code #	Account Title
441	Interdenominational Cooperation Funds
442	General Administration Fund
443	Jurisdictional Administration Fund
444	Area & Conference Administration Fund
445	District Administration Fund

CONNECTIONAL CLERGY SUPPORT

Code #	Account Title
461	Pension CRSP/CPP
462	Pension: Paid to Conference
463	District Superintendents' Fund
464	Episcopal Fund
465	Equitable Compensation Fund

LOCAL CHURCH CLERGY SUPPORT

Code #	Account Title
501	Base Compensation: Pastor
502	Base Compensation: Associate
503	Housing & Utilities: Pastor
504	Housing & Utilities: Associate
507	Accountable Reimbursements: Pastor
508	Accountable Reimbursements: Associate
509	Other Cash Allowances: Pastor
510	Other Cash Allowances: Associate
511	Base Compensation: Deacon(s)
512	Housing & Utilities: Deacon(s)
513	Accountable Reimbursements: Deacon(s)
514	Other Cash Allowances: Deacon(s)

LOCAL CHURCH EXPENSES

Code #	Account Title
521	Diaconal Minister/Deacon Salaries
522	Diaconal Minister/Deacon Fringe Benefits/Expenses
523	Other Staff Salaries
524	Other Staff Fringe Benefits/Expenses
525	Nurture & Membership
526	Church & Society
527	Church Education
528	Evangelism
529	Missions
530	Stewardship
532	Worship
533-538	Program Expenses
539	Other Program Expenses
540	Finance Committee
541	Office Expense
542	Repairs & Maintenance
543	Insurance
544	Church Utilities
545-548	Operating Expenses
549	Other Operating Expense
550	Interest Paid on Debt
551	Capital Improvements

- Arrange with the bank to have them send you a receipted copy of the deposit from the bank.

- Each week, check the totals on the CASH RECEIPTS VOUCHER, the deposit slip, the bank receipt, and the tape for agreement. Discuss any discrepancies with the counters, the bank, and the financial secretary until they are cleared up.

Cash Receipts Journal

Using your CHART OF ACCOUNTS, set up the CASH RECEIPTS JOURNAL. The purpose of the CASH RECEIPTS JOURNAL is to record and balance by deposit and by category all funds received. Note that the CASH RECEIPTS JOURNAL is laid out left to right, so the pre-printed headings following the DATE and DEPOSITED IN BANK columns are in the same sequence as the CASH RECEIPTS VOUCHER. You may head up additional columns or paste in new headings as needed to fit your particular situation.

Cash Receipts Journal "How to"

- Number the journal sheets sequentially and by month to make future referencing and posting easier.

- Date the line on the CASH RECEIPTS JOURNAL to agree with the date on the CASH RECEIPTS VOUCHER you are working from.

- Under the DEPOSITED IN BANK column, enter the amount from the TOTAL column on the CASH RECEIPTS VOUCHER.

- Under the columns designated for each type of income (BUDGET, BENEVOLENCES, INTEREST & DIVIDEND, SALE OF CHURCH ASSETS, BUILDING USE FEES, CONTRIBUTIONS, & RENTALS, FUNDRAISERS, CAPITAL CAMPAIGNS, OTHER), enter the totals for each type of income from the CASH RECEIPTS VOUCHER.

- Check off (✓) each item on the CASH RECEIPTS VOUCHER as you post it to the CASH RECEIPTS JOURNAL sheet.

CASH RECEIPTS JOURNAL

CHURCH *FIRST UNITED METHODIST CHURCH*

MONTH/YEAR *Sept. 2005*

	DATE	CASH RECEIPTS VOUCHER NO.	DEPOSITED IN BANK	ENVELOPES, PLEDGES, & TITHES	LOOSE PLATE OFFERING	CHURCH SCHOOL	OTHER INCOME		DESIGNATED GIFTS AND SPECIAL OFFERINGS	
							DESCRIPTION	AMOUNT	DESCRIPTION	AMOUNT
1	9 5	36	810 00	710 00	20 00	30 00			World Communion (413)	40 00
2									Memorials (254)	10 00
3	9 12	37	750 00	700 00	25 00	20 00			" (254)	5 00
4	9 15	38	50 00				Rent (324)	50 00		
5	9 19	39	800 00	750 00	25 00	25 00				
6	9 26	40	825 00	725 00	30 00	30 00			Memorials (254)	100 00
7									Ch. Ed. Sun (415)	40 00
8	9 30	41	100 00				Dividend (324)	100 00		
9			# 3435 00	# 2885 00	# 100 00		Sept. Totals	# 150 00		
10										
11			#	#	#		YEAR-TO-DATE PREVIOUS MONTH			
12										
13			#	#	#		YEAR-TO-DATE TOTALS			
14										
15							Recapitulation — For the General			
16			Acct. No. 321	322	323		Ledger or (Treasurer's Report)			
17			# 2885 00	# 100 00	# 105 00		Rent (324)	# 50 00	World Communion (413)	40 00
18							Dividend (324)	100 00	Ch. Ed. Sun (415)	40 00
19									Memorials (254)	115 00
20			# 2885 00	# 100 00	# 105 00			# 150 00		# 195 00
21										
22										
23										
24										
25										
26										
27										
28										

RECORDS RETENTION GUIDELINES

The length of time that you should keep the financial, tax, and personnel records of the church varies with the type of record. It may also vary in your state. Listed below are the number of years that you are required to keep records in accordance with appropriate federal regulations. You may want to ask your State Department of Revenue if there are any records that they require to be retained longer than stated here.

Financial/Tax Records	Retention Period
General Ledger/Journal Entries	Permanent
Minutes of Church Council	Permanent
Minutes of Trustees	Permanent
Audit Reports	Permanent
Expense/Payables Ledger	Permanent
Receivable Ledger	6 Years
Bank Statements	6 Years
Bank Reconciliations	6 Years
Deposit Slips	6 Years

Cash Receipts Journal	6 Years
Cash Disbursements Summary	6 Years
Canceled Checks	6 Years
Inventory Records	6 Years
Not-for-Profit Reports	Permanent
State and County Tax Bills	Permanent
Federal and State Income Tax Returns	Permanent
Withholding Returns	4 Years
Sales and Use Tax Returns	3 Years

Payroll/Personnel Records	
Current Employee Folders	All Records from start
Former Employee Folder	4 Years
Employee Earnings Records/ Payroll Spread Sheets	4 Years
Time Cards/Payroll Journal	4 Years
Rejected Applications	2 Years

- On each line, total across all the columns to the right of the DEPOSITED IN BANK column. The total of these columns must agree with the entry in the DEPOSITED IN BANK column on that line.

- Make separate line entries for each CASH RECEIPTS VOUCHER you receive. If several bank accounts are involved, adapt the sheet to fit your needs.

- Enter the previous month's year-to-date totals. Add and enter totals for the year to date.

- Study the completed example of the CASH RECEIPTS JOURNAL on the previous page. Examine the recapitulation at the bottom of the sheet. The entries for the month are summarized by account numbers. **These summary amounts are the figures that you will enter on your monthly Treasurer's Report.**

- If your record keeping requirements are simple, the TREASURER'S REPORT will serve as your GENERAL LEDGER.

How to Change an Entry

The standard rule for changing any entry already made is to strike once through the incorrect entry, enter the correction above or below, and *initial* the change. *This is important!* Also date the change, especially if it is made at a later date. If dollar amounts are changed, re-add and change subtotals and totals.

- File the bank deposit slips by date. You will need them for your bank statement reconciliation and any communication with bank(s). **See the chart on this page for recommendations on record retention.**

Cash Disbursements—
General Instructions

- Create or secure a supporting document for each check you or other authorized persons write and post.

- After posting from the checkbook, write the check number on the voucher, invoice, purchase order, or other document from which you make payment. This confirms that the "bill" has been paid and establishes an *audit trail* for reconciliation and control.

- Bind all paid documents in a "Vouchers-and-Invoices-Paid Binder." Use a binder or folder with alphabetical pockets so that you can quickly research these documents by vendor in order to respond to billing questions or to assist in the budgeting process.

- Place unpaid vouchers and bills in a pocket in front of the binder or folder until you pay them.

- For predetermined expenses such as salaries, the supporting document is the approved church budget or a schedule adopted by the church council.

- Confirm that all bills and vouchers submitted for payment carry the signature and approval date of the person/s designated by the committee on finance and/or the church council to authorize disbursements for the church.

Who May Approve Payments?

Establish among all the church financial leaders (the treasurer, the finance committee, the church council/administrative board, and the pastor-in-charge) a clear understanding of the procedure for approving payments, and put it in writing. Refer improperly authorized vouchers to the committee on finance chairperson and the pastor.

- Use the three descriptive columns on the left of the CASH DISBURSEMENT JOURNAL sheet to record each check written. The check stub or invoice will provide the detailed information that is needed. Post entries sequentially from the checkbook.

Cash Disbursement Journal Sheet—Examples of Entries

Example 1. An invoice is received for the church phone bill in the amount of $38.50 as of September 15.

The treasurer knows that the budget provides for this and that the CHART OF ACCOUNTS shows that account 544 (Church Utilities) should be charged. Assuming the treasurer writes the check on September 1, the CASH DISBURSEMENTS JOURNAL entry would read like this:

	DATE	PAYEE	CHECK NO.	(1) CASH CREDIT AMOUNT	(2) PAYROLL TAXES WITHHELD CREDIT (DEBIT) CODE AMOUNT	O CI CO	(7) APITAL PENSES DEBIT AMOUNT	(8) PROGRAM EXPENSE CODE DEBIT AMOUNT	(9) OPERATING EXPENSE CODE DEBIT AMOUNT	(10) DESIGNATED GIFTS AND SPECIAL OFFERINGS CODE DEBIT AMOUNT
1	Sept. 1	Central Bell Telephone	1024	38 50					544 38 50	
2										
3										
4										

Example 2. A further look at the budget and the payable records indicates it is time to write the pastor's end-of-the-month salary check.

—The pastor is to receive $800 salary on the fifteenth and thirtieth of each month, according to the minutes of the church council, and the treasurer is further authorized to withhold $66 to pay the pastor's share of medical insurance premiums and $24 for the pastor's personal pension contribution. In addition, the pastor receives a monthly cash allowance of $55 for travel expenses.

—NOTE: For future reference, create a spreadsheet of such payments and deductions each pay period on each pastor and employee. (See pages 31-32.)

—The columns numbered 1-14 are designed to allow posting of the total amount paid and the distribution among the accounts involved. The entry would then look like this:

	DATE	PAYEE	CHECK NO.	(1) CASH CREDIT AMOUNT	(2) PAYROLL TAXES WITHHELD CREDIT (DEBIT)* CODE	(2) AMOUNT	(3) OTHER PAYROLL DEDUCTIONS CREDIT (DEBIT)* CODE	(3) AMOUNT	B|	DN	(6) CLERGY SUPPORT DEBIT CODE	(6) AMOUNT	CODE	C EX
1	Sept. 30	J. C. Smith	1025	765			218	24			501	800		
2							216	66			509	55		
3														
4														

—For illustration purposes, in column 3, account **216** (Group Insurance Withholding) equals health insurance and account **218** (Employee/Pastor Reserves/Pension) equals the personal pension contribution.

—In column 6, account **501** (Pastor Base Compensation) equals salary and account **509** (Other Cash Allowances: Pastor) equals the cash allowance.

—Columns 1-3 are credit columns, with 2 and 3 for deductions set by the schedule adopted by the church council.

—The amounts in the credit columns 1-3 must cross-total to the amounts in the debit columns 4-14.

— In many churches, columns 2 and 3 will not be used. Where they are, you (the treasurer) will later write a check to the bank, government agency, or pension board. You will then enter the amount of the deduction you paid in column 2 or 3, indicating a *debit* by placing brackets [ ] around the debit figure.

—At any time the *net* year-to-date total of columns 2 and 3 should show the amount payable in these categories. (See footnote on Cash Disbursements Journal sheet.)

NOTE: **Cash allowances** (for travel or anything else) are treated as taxable income and the pastor must account for them on IRS 1040, Schedule A. However, if travel expenses are part of an **Accountable Reimbursement Plan**, then vouchers for travel expenses are required of the pastor and the appropriate expense account would be # 507 Accountable Reimbursements: Pastor. To avoid confusion, do not combine Accountable Reimbursable Plan payments with the regular paycheck.

Example 3. The *Discipline* indicates that World Service, Conference Benevolences, and other conference apportionments and special benevolence gifts shall be paid monthly.

—The treasurer notes from the CASH RECEIPTS VOUCHER that $50 was received on a budgeted Advance special. There is also a statement from the conference treasurer or district superintendent of the amount of World Service, conference benevolences, and other apportionments due each month. The monthly check might be entered as follows:

	DATE	PAYEE	CHECK NO.	(1) CASH CREDIT AMOUNT	PAY V CRE CODE	ER PAYROLL EDUCTIONS DIT (DEBIT)* AMOUNT	(3) CODE	(4) BENEVOLENCES DEBIT AMOUNT	(5) CONNECTIONAL ADMINISTRATION CODE DEBIT AMOUNT	(6) CLERGY SUPPORT CODE DEBIT AMOUNT	C E> CODE
1	Sept. 30	Ann. Conf. Treasurer	1030	453 50			419	50 —	442	36 —	464	50 —	
2							401	225 —				
3							402	92 50				
4											

—The $50 in account 419 (Conference Advance Specials) is in column 4 because this Conference Advance Special was a budgeted item. If a nonbudgeted Advance Special has been received, it would be entered in column 10.
—In column 6, account 464 is used for Episcopal Fund Support, and in column 5, account 442 is used for General Administration Fund.
—In column 4, account 401 is used for World Service, account 402 for Conference Benevolences, and account 418 is used for Conference Advance specials.

Closing the Cash Disbursement Journal

● At the end of each month, total each column. The total of all debit columns, 4-14, must equal the net credit total of columns 1, 2, and 3. Rule off the totals for the month at the bottom of the page for posting to your monthly **Treasurer's Report**.

● Study the complete example of the CASH DISBURSEMENTS JOURNAL below. Examine the recapitulation at the bottom of the sheet. There the entries for the month are summarized by account numbers. You will later enter these summary amounts on the monthly TREASURER'S REPORT.

CASH DISBURSEMENTS JOURNAL
CHURCH: FIRST
MONTH/YEAR: Sept. 2005
PAGE NO. _____

DATE	PAYEE	CHECK NO.	(1) CASH CREDIT AMOUNT	(2) PAYROLL TAXES WITHHELD CODE/AMT	(3) OTHER PAYROLL DEDUCTIONS CODE/AMT	(4) BENEVOLENCES CODE/AMT	(5) CONNECTIONAL ADMINISTRATION CODE/AMT	(6) CLERGY SUPPORT CODE/AMT	(7) CAPITAL EXPENSES CODE/AMT	(8) PROGRAM EXPENSE CODE/AMT	(9) OPERATING EXPENSE CODE/AMT	(10) DESIGNATED GIFTS AND SPECIAL OFFERINGS CODE/AMT
Sept. 1	Benson Hardware Co.	1016	43 50								542 / 43 50	
8	Central Arts/Crafts Co	1017	31 40							532 / 31 40		
	City Electric Co.	1018	87 10								544 / 87 10	
	Southern Gas Co.	1019	58 80								544 / 58 80	
15	Sandra Adams	1020	346 71	212 / 29 29							523 / 390 —	
				213 / 14 —								
	Joseph Whitcomb	1021	333 71	212 / 29 29							523 / 390 —	
				213 / 27 —								
	J. C. Smith	1022	757 50			218 / 24 —		501 / 800 00				
						216 / 47 50		509 / 29 00				
	Jordan Music Co.	1023	22 30							532 / 22 30		
30	Central Bell Telephone	1024	38 50								544 / 38 50	
	J. C. Smith	1025	765 —			218 / 24 —		501 / 800 —				
						216 / 66 —		509 / 55 —				
	Sandra Adams	1026	346 71	212 / 29 29							523 / 390 —	
				213 / 14 —								
	Joseph Whitcomb	1027	333 71	212 / 29 29							523 / 390 —	
				213 / 27 —								
	General Board Pensions	1028	412 40		461 / (48 —)			462 / 224 —			524 / 140 40	
	Cokesbury	1029	63 50							532 / 63 50		
	Ann. Conf. Treasurer	1030	388 50			401 / 225 — 462 / 36 —						410 / 15 —
						402 / 112 50						
	SEPTEMBER TOTALS		4027 34	199 16	113 50	337 50	36 —	1908 —		117 20	1928 30	15 —

RECAPITULATION FOR TREASURER'S REPORT (GENERAL LEDGER)

				212 / 117 16	218 / 48 —	401 / 225 — 462 / 36 —		501 / 1600 —		532 / 117 20	542 / 43 50	410 / 15 —
				213 / 82 00	216 / 113 50	402 / 112 50		509 / 84 —			544 / 184 40	
					461 / (48 —)			462 / 224 —			523 / 156 0 —	
											524 / 140 40	
				199 16	113 50	337 50	36 —	1908 —		117 20	1928 30	15 —

PREPARED AND EDITED BY THE GENERAL COUNCIL ON FINANCE AND ADMINISTRATION. NO. 43051B ● PAYMENT OF TAXES WITHHELD AND OTHER PAYROLL DEDUCTIONS TO BE SHOWN IN BRACKETS ( ) IN THESE COLUMNS, WHEN TOTALING, SUBTRACT AMOUNTS IN BRACKETS. © 1976 THE UNITED METHODIST PUBLISHING HOUSE   PRINTED IN U.S.A.

Monthly Treasurer's Cash Report

The church treasurer prepares a TREASURER'S REPORT on a regular basis, usually monthly, and makes it available to the committee on finance and the church council (each time they meet), to the charge conference (when it meets), and to the pastor and other local church officers (as needed).

Depending on many factors—the size of your church and its budget, the number and complexity of financial transactions, the amount of detail requested by the committee on finance—the TREASURER'S REPORT may vary greatly in length and the amount of specific information it contains.

A sample model for a TREASURER'S REPORT is provided on the next four pages. Study this model and feel free to condense or expand it to reflect your needs and your own CHART OF ACCOUNTS.

TREASURER'S CASH REPORT

Church_____

For the period from _____, 20_____ to _____, 20_____

CODE	ACCOUNT	ANNUAL BUDGET	THIS MONTH	YEAR TO DATE	YTD% OF BUDGET
	CASH BALANCE—				
121	Beginning of Period		_____	_____	
	RECEIPTS				
	Annual Operating Budget & Benevolences				
	Giving Funding Sources:				
321	Received from Pledgers	_____	_____	_____	_____
325	Received from Non-Pledgers/Identified Givers	_____	_____	_____	_____
331	Received from unidentified Givers	_____	_____	_____	_____
	RECEIPTS FROM OTHER SOURCES:				
335	Interest	_____	_____	_____	_____
341	Sale of Church Assets	_____	_____	_____	_____
345	Building Use Fees, Contributions, & Rentals	_____	_____	_____	_____
351	Fundraisers/Other:	_____	_____	_____	_____
	_____	_____	_____	_____	_____
	RECEIPTS FOR CAPITAL AND OTHER SPECIAL PROJECTS:				
361	Capital Campaigns	_____	_____	_____	_____
371	Human Relations Day	_____	_____	_____	_____
372	One Great Hour of Sharing	_____	_____	_____	_____
373	Peace with Justice Sunday	_____	_____	_____	_____
374	Native American Ministries Sunday	_____	_____	_____	_____
375	World Communion	_____	_____	_____	_____
376	U.M. Student Day	_____	_____	_____	_____
365	Memorial/Endowment/Bequests	_____	_____	_____	_____
391	Other Sources and Projects:	_____	_____	_____	_____
	_____	_____	_____	_____	_____
	RECEIPTS FROM DISTRICT(S), ANNUAL CONFERENCE(S), JURISDICTIONAL CONFERENCE(S), GENERAL CHURCH AND/OR OTHER INSTITUTIONAL SOURCES OUTSIDE THE LOCAL CHURCH:				
381	Equitable Compensation Funds received by Church or Pastor	_____	_____	_____	_____
385	Advance Special or Apportioned Funds Received by Church	_____	_____	_____	_____
391	Other:	_____	_____	_____	_____
	_____	_____	_____	_____	_____
	TOTAL RECEIPTS	XXXX	_____	_____	XXXX
	TOTAL AVAILABLE FUNDS	XXXX	_____	_____	XXXX

TREASURER'S CASH REPORT CONTINUED—PAGE 2

Church_____

For the period from _____, 20_____ to _____, 20_____

CODE	ACCOUNT	ANNUAL BUDGET	THIS MONTH	YEAR TO DATE	YTD% OF BUDGET
	DISBURSEMENTS				
	BUDGETED DISBURSEMENTS:				
	Benevolences:				
401	World Service	____	____	____	____
402	Conference Benevolences	____	____	____	____
403	Ministerial Education Fund	____	____	____	____
404	Black College Fund	____	____	____	____
405	Africa University Fund	____	____	____	____
406	General Advance Specials	____	____	____	____
407	World Service Special Gifts	____	____	____	____
408	Youth Service Fund	____	____	____	____
409	Human Relations Day Fund	____	____	____	____
410	One Great Hour of Sharing Fund	____	____	____	____
411	Peace with Justice Fund	____	____	____	____
412	Native American Ministries Fund	____	____	____	____
413	World Communion Fund	____	____	____	____
414	U.M. Student Day Fund	____	____	____	____
419	Conference Advance Specials	____	____	____	____
420-424	Other Benevolences:				
____	_____	____	____	____	____
____	_____	____	____	____	____
	Total Benevolences	____	____	____	____
441-445	**Connectional Administration Funds:**				
____	_____	____	____	____	____
____	_____	____	____	____	____
	Total Connectional Administration	____	____	____	____
	Clergy Support:				
461-465	Connectional Clergy Support	____	____	____	____
____	_____	____	____	____	____
____	_____	____	____	____	____
____					
	Local Clergy Support:				
	Base Compensation	____	____	____	____
501	Pastor	____	____	____	____
502	Associate(s)	____	____	____	____
511	Deacon(s)	____	____	____	____
	Utilities and Other Housing-related Allowances:				
503	Pastor	____	____	____	____
504	Associate(s)	____	____	____	____
512	Deacon(s)	____	____	____	____

TREASURER'S CASH REPORT CONTINUED—PAGE 3

Church_____

For the period from _____, 20_____ to _____, 20_____

CODE	ACCOUNT	ANNUAL BUDGET	THIS MONTH	YEAR TO DATE	YTD% OF BUDGET
	Accountable Reimbursements:				
507	Pastor				
508	Associate(s)				
513	Deacon(s)				
	Other Cash Allowances:				
509	Pastor				
510	Associate(s)				
514	Deacon(s)				
	Total Clergy Support				
	Diaconal Ministers' Compensation:				
521	Base Compensation				
522	Employee Benefits				
	Other Lay Employees' Compensation:				
523	Base Compensation				
524	Employee Benefits				
	Program Expense:				
525	Nurture & Membership Ministries				
526	Church and Society/Community Volunteers				
527	Education/Church School				
528	Evangelism				
529	Missions				
530	Stewardship				
532	Worship				
533-538	Higher Education/Campus Ministry				
533-538	Religion and Race				
533-538	Status and Role of Women				
533-538	Outreach Ministries				
533-538	Christian Unity/Inter-religious Concerns				
533-538	Witness Ministries				
539	Other Program Expenses				
	Operating Expense:				
540	Finance Committee				
541	Office Expenses				
542	Repairs & Property Maintenance				
543	Insurance (property, liability, worker's compensation)				
544	Church Utilities				
549	Other Operating Expense				
550	Interest Paid on Debt				

TREASURER'S CASH REPORT CONTINUED—PAGE 4

Church_____

For the period from _____, 20_____ to _____, 20_____

CODE	ACCOUNT	ANNUAL BUDGET	THIS MONTH	YEAR TO DATE	YTD% OF BUDGET
220-221	Debt Retirement	_____	_____	_____	_____
551	Capital Improvements	_____	_____	_____	_____
	Total Program and Operating Expense	_____	_____	_____	_____
	Total Budgeted Disbursements				
212-219	Net of Payroll Deductions (Withheld)/Paid Out		(_____)	(_____)	
	Net Budgeted Disbursements	_____	_____	_____	_____
250-290	Unbudgeted Disbursements: **Designated Gifts and Unbudgeted Special Offerings Disbursed:**				
_____	_____	XXXX	_____	_____	XXXX
_____	_____	XXXX	_____	_____	XXXX
_____	_____	XXXX	_____	_____	XXXX
_____	_____	XXXX	_____	_____	XXXX
	Total Designated Gifts and Unbudgeted Special Offerings Disbursed	XXXX	_____	_____	XXXX
	TOTAL DISBURSEMENTS	XXXX	_____	_____	XXXX
	TOTAL CASH BALANCE, END OF PERIOD (Total Available Funds, less Total Disbursements)	XXXX	_____	_____	XXXX

Whatever model you use, the TREASURER'S REPORT should include these elements:
- —The name of the church
- —The time period covered by the report
- —A breakdown of receipts for the month (or period of the report)
- —A breakdown of disbursements for the month (or period of the report)
- —Year-to-date receipts and disbursements
- —Annual budget for budgeted receipts and disbursements
- —A comparison (percentage or otherwise) between the budgeted amounts and the actual receipts and disbursements for the year to date.

The TREASURER'S REPORT is a summary of all the church's financial transactions for a specified period of time. This means that if a church has more than one treasurer, for example, a separate treasurer will need either to prepare a separate report or to work with the other treasurers in preparing a joint report. If separate reports are prepared by various treasurers, they should work together to prepare a consolidated report at least at the end of each year.

Since the report is a summary of financial transactions for a particular month and for the year to date broken down by categories, it can double as the General Ledger for many churches; that is, the function usually served by a GENERAL LEDGER in a financial record system will be served by a file of monthly TREASURER'S REPORTS prepared with this form. For churches that have a complex account structure, a separate GENERAL LEDGER will probably still be required, but many churches may find the extra step of maintaining a GENERAL LEDGER unnecessary.

Preparing the Monthly Treasurer's Cash Report
- Gather the source documents you need:
  - —Approved budget for the year
  - —CHART OF ACCOUNTS
  - —CASH RECEIPTS JOURNAL for the month
  - —CASH DISBURSEMENTS JOURNAL for the month
  - —TREASURER'S CASH REPORT from the previous month (if the report you are preparing is not for the first month of the year)

- NEW TREASURERS' NOTE: Before you complete the YEAR-TO-DATE column of your monthly report, confirm that the account classifications of the previous report match. If you have revised your CHART OF ACCOUNTS and the format of your report to match it, then remember to re-sort the YEAR-TO-DATE totals from the previous month report to your new report format.

- Enter the amounts from your church's approved budget on the appropriate lines in the column headed ANNUAL BUDGET.

- In the column headed CODE, enter the account numbers from your CHART OF ACCOUNTS. The account numbers shown on the sample match the CHART OF ACCOUNTS on page 18.

- Enter the appropriate amounts on the line CASH BALANCE—BEGINNING OF PERIOD.
  —In the THIS MONTH column, the figure you enter should be the same as the TOTAL CASH BALANCE, END OF PERIOD from your previous report. It should also be the same as the balance from your checkbook (plus any savings account or investment balances) at the beginning of the month. In the YEAR-TO-DATE column, the beginning cash balance is the balance at the beginning of your church's fiscal year—usually January 1. *This figure remains the same throughout the year.*

Recording "This Month" Totals
- Reconcile the bank statement with the checkbook. (See page 33 for instructions.).

- Prepare the monthly recapitulation on your CASH RECEIPTS JOURNAL and your CASH DISBURSEMENTS JOURNAL (see pages 21–24).

- Enter the amounts from the receipts and disbursement recapitulations in the appropriate spaces in the THIS MONTH column of your report.

- Add the figures entered in the THIS MONTH column of the report form to obtain the various subtotals and totals indicated on the form (TOTAL BUDGETED INCOME, TOTAL UNBUDGETED INCOME, TOTAL RECEIPTS, TOTAL BENEVOLENCES, etc.).

- Check for transcription errors. Compare totals with the corresponding subtotals and totals on the CASH RECEIPTS JOURNAL and CASH DISBURSE-MENTS JOURNAL sheets. If your totals match, this confirms that you made no errors in transferring figures from one form to the other.

● Note that the way lines are indented on the TREA-SURER'S REPORT form are intended to assist you in identifying the figures that should be added together, but take care—it's tricky. For example, to obtain the TOTAL AVAILABLE FUNDS figure, add the CASH BALANCE, BEGINNING OF PERIOD figure to the TOTAL RECEIPTS figure. (The TOTAL RECEIPTS figure is the result of adding the figures for TOTAL BUDGETED INCOME and TOTAL UNBUD-GETED INCOME.)

● Subtract the amount of TOTAL DISBURSEMENTS from the TOTAL AVAILABLE FUNDS figure, and enter the difference in the TOTAL CASH BALANCE, END OF PERIOD line. This figure should agree with your checkbook balance, plus savings and other investment balances reflected in this report at the end of the reporting period.

SPECIAL INSTRUCTIONS
1. Capital Improvements

Under the heading BUDGETED DISBURSEMENTS, the space provided for reporting CAPITAL IMPROVEMENTS should be used if such improvements are paid from regular budgeted income. CAPITAL IMPROVEMENTS include the cost of new property and buildings, major purchases of new equipment or furnishings (organs or other musical instruments, heating and cooling equipment, kitchen equipment, audiovisual equipment, furniture), and major renovation.

If money for CAPITAL IMPROVEMENTS is raised separately from the regular budget (that is, if contributors are asked to give money specifically earmarked for those purposes), both the receipts and the expenditures should be reported in the underlined section of the report form.

2. Apportionments

Beginning with BENEVOLENCES and continuing through CONNECTIONAL CLERGY SUPPORT, much of what you report will be payments on apportionments. The number of accounts you use and their titles will depend on your annual conference. You should show a separate line on the report for each separate apportionment in your annual conference.

3. Payroll Withholding

If your church withholds amounts for taxes or other purposes from any salaries it pays, be aware that laws and regulations affecting withholding may change. The treasurer is responsible for securing current, accurate information on taxes and government regulations and confirming that information annually. See "Payroll, Taxes, and Government Issues" for helpful resources available from the General Council of Finance and Administration on page 32

If the amounts withheld have already been disbursed to the Internal Revenue Service, state or city revenue agencies, banks, insurance companies, or other appropriate agencies, no special reporting is required on this form. If, however, there is an amount that has been withheld but not yet disbursed, the amount should be entered on the line that reads NET OF PAYROLL DEDUCTIONS (WITHHELD)/PAID OUT. This amount should then be subtracted from the TOTAL BUDGETED DISBURSEMENTS, and the difference should be entered as the NET BUDGETED DISBURSE-MENTS. It is this net figure that should be added to the line for TOTAL DESIGNATED GIFTS AND UNBUDGETED SPECIAL OFFERINGS DISBURSED to yield the amount of TOTAL DISBURSEMENTS.

It is worthwhile to examine the reason for this procedure. When a salary is paid, the total amount of that salary for the pay period is charged against a budget expense account. However, the check written to the employee is for a smaller amount, the salary less deductions. Unless this difference is taken into account, the checkbook balance and the TOTAL CASH BALANCE, END OF PERIOD line on the TREASURER'S REPORT will not agree.

4. Use a Spreadsheet to Keep Track of Payroll Withholding

A payroll spreadsheet such as the one illustrated on the next page will help you organize each employee's payroll withholding and organize the data you need for your monthly TREASURER'S REPORT as well as your quarterly reports to government offices. (A reproducible master is provided on page 56.)

Prepare a spreadsheet like this for each payroll and keep them in a notebook (or a computer file) for use at the end of each month and quarter. Each time you issue paychecks, use one of these sheets to keep track of all the exclusions, deductions and subtotals. Num-

Payroll Spread Sheet

Church _FIRST_   Page _3_

Month/Year _3/05_   Payroll Number _3_

Name / Distribution	JOHN SMITH		MARTHA JONES		GEORGE BROWN								Total	
Gross Comp.	150	00	157	00	55	00							362	00	523
Excludable Fringe														
Group Insurance	(25	00)	—		—								(25	00)	216
Medical	(10	00)	(15	00)	—								(25	00)	218
Dependent Care	—		(40	00)	—								(40	00)	218
Life Insurance	—		—		—								—		
Pension	(5	00)	—		—								(5	00)	218
Reportable Comp.	110	00	102	00	55	00							267	00	TO 941
With/Deduction														
Social Security Tax	(6	82)	(6	32)	(3	41)							(16	55)	212
Medicare Tax	(1	60)	(1	48)	(80)								(3	88)	219
Fed. Inc. Tax	(4	00)	(2	00)	—								(6	00)	213
State Inc. Tax	(3	30)	(3	06)	(1	65)							(8	01)	214
Local Inc. Tax	(1	10)	(1	02)	(55)								(2	67)	215
Other Deductions														
CREDIT UNION	(5	00)	—		—								(5	00)	217
Net Compensation (Paycheck)	88	18	88	12	48	59							224	89	150

ber the sheets from the first of the year, then you can easily designate on your copies of government forms which payrolls they cover (Payroll 1, 2, 3, etc.).

For each employee/pastor, start with the gross pay earned whether hourly (dollars per hour multiplied by the hours worked) or salaried (fixed salary for the period). Then record the amount(s) of each exclusion that has been approved for that person. Some exclusions may be fixed amounts, others may be based on a percentage of base pay. Subtract all of these exclusions from the gross pay to obtain the employee's REPORTABLE COMPENSATION, which you report on the employee's Form W-2. Use reportable compensation to calculate Social Security and Medicare withholding (except for pastors) and to enter the tax table figures for federal and state withholding.

Using the number of exemptions claimed on the per-son's most recent W-4, find the amounts to be withheld for that pay period. In the case of income tax withholding, be sure to include any additional amount that the person has requested on their W-4 or the state equivalent of the W-4. Also be sure to deduct any special withholding that the person has requested and the church has agreed to, such as credit union savings, U.S. savings bonds, disability insurance, court-ordered garnishees, etc. Subtract all of these deductions from the REPORTABLE COMPENSATION and the result should be the actual amount of the paycheck.

Make totals across the page for all the paychecks you write for the payroll and you will have the summary data you need to post to your TREASURER'S REPORT or GENERAL LEDGER. Include the CHART OF ACCOUNT code numbers to help with posting and later audit reviews.

Payroll, Taxes, and Government Issues
No Matter What Size Church You Are, *Read This!*

Churches, both large and small, are experiencing difficulty with the federal and state tax authorities because they do not understand that major changes have occurred in the past few years regarding their potential tax liability and their reporting responsibilities. The days of, "we're too small" and "the dollars aren't large enough to matter" are now gone. Tiny organizations are being penalized for failure to report their quarterly payroll obligations even though it might be only a few dollars. The minimum penalty plus interest can be substantial. Gone also are the days when the part-time custodian made too little, or worked too infrequently, to take out tax withholding or Social Security. Even if you do not have an employee, which is unlikely for even the smallest church, you still have a reporting responsibility for payments made to independent persons, such as a lawyer, accountant, painter, roofer, or plumber.

The treasurer is the officer of the church who is responsible for compiling and certifying the accuracy of the data to the federal, state, and local tax offices. Important information to assist the treasurer in meeting this responsibility is provided by the following general agencies:

Available from GCFA at www.gcfa.org:
- **Clergy Tax Information** (*new each year*)
- **The Local Church Audit Guide**
- Changes made by the Committee on Official Forms and Records, including changes to Tables I, II, and III, are available at **www.gcfa.org** or by contacting your district superintendent.

Available from Wespath.org
- **Pastoral Compensation, Benefits, and Support** (*new each year*)

The Treasurer's Cash Report Continued
Recording Year-to-date Totals

- In the first month of any year, the THIS MONTH and YEAR-TO-DATE figures will be identical.

- For subsequent months, add the THIS MONTH figures to the YEAR-TO-DATE figures, which appear on the previous month's report. This will yield the new YEAR-TO-DATE amounts.
  —REMEMBER: The CASH BALANCE—BEGINNING OF PERIOD stays the same in the YEAR-TO-DATE column for the entire year).

- Be sure all YEAR-TO-DATE amounts from the previous report are reflected in the new report; carry forward YEAR-TO-DATE figures from the previous month's report for any accounts that had no THIS MONTH amounts.

- Add the figures in the YEAR-TO-DATE column to determine subtotals and totals, following the same procedures used for the THIS MONTH column.

- The TOTAL CASH BALANCE, END OF PERIOD amount should be the same in both columns.

Comparing the Actual to Budget

The last column on the report allows you to show how actual expenditures compare with the approved budget. **This can be done in one of two ways:**

1. Calculate the percentage of the annual approved budget represented by the YEAR-TO-DATE amount for each budgeted item and enter that percentage in this column; or

2. Subtract the YEAR-TO-DATE amount from the annual approved budget and enter the difference in this column. If you choose this method, you will want to change the column heading to "BUDGET BALANCE."

Available Cash

Following the TOTAL CASH BALANCE, THE END OF PERIOD line is a section of the form that will enable you to determine and report how much of the cash balance is available for use—that is, not designated for some specific purpose. From time to time churches receive special offerings or gifts designated by their donor for a specific purpose. As a matter of principle, these monies should be disbursed for the

The Bank Statement

The treasurer or a member of the committee on finance should reconcile bank statements promptly upon receipt, prior to preparation of the monthly Treasurer's Report. The person who reconciles the bank statement should not sign disbursement checks.

Reconciling the Bank Statement, Step by Step

1. Arrange the paid checks returned with your bank statement in check number order and arrange the deposit slips in date sequence.

2. Check off on your checkbook record and last month's reconcilement each entry that matches a paid check or deposit.

3. List and total the checks outstanding, including prior month's (all checks not matching a paid check in step 2).

4. Enter and subtract from checkbook balance all bank statement charges not previously entered (service charges, etc.). *Remember to enter bank charges in the Cash Disbursements Journal.*

5. Starting with the new balance from bank statement, add the deposits and credits not yet shown on the bank statement and deduct all the checks that are outstanding. Be sure that the resulting balance agrees with the checkbook balance. When it does, the reconciliation process is complete.

6. Reconcile to the Total Cash Balance, End of Period on your Treasurer's Report.

purpose for which they were intended as quickly as possible. There will be occasions, however, when a reporting period will close with such monies still on hand. Enter in the two spaces provided the total of such special offerings and designated gifts received but not yet disbursed. Subtract the Total Designated Gifts and Unbudgeted Special Offerings on Hand from the Total Cash Balance, End of Period. Enter the resulting difference as Net Available Cash.

Reporting to the Charge Conference and the District Superintendent

The treasurer's work in establishing the Chart of Accounts and the format for the monthly Treasurer's Report and in maintaining complete and accurate records of receipts and disbursements will help the committee on finance, the trustees, and the auditors complete their annual reports to the charge conference and the district superintendent.

Available at www.gcfa.org are reproducible masters of the three charge conference forms developed for use by United Methodist congregations by the General Council on Finance and Administration:

—Annual Report of the Committee on Finance
—Annual Report of Trustees
—Fund Balance Report

These forms have been reviewed to meet the requirements of the *Book of Discipline* 2016. Churches or districts may wish to collect additional information which can be included with these core reports as addenda.

Your review of these reports will help you identify ways to set up your Chart of Accounts and your monthly Treasurer's Report to make completing these reports easier and more accurate.

Reporting to the Annual Conference

The treasurer's record-keeping will also facilitate the pastor's work in completing The Local Church Report to the Annual Conference, Table 1 (Financial Report) and Table 3 (Financial Report). The ease of completing this report is directly related to the format of your Chart of Accounts and your Treasurer's Cash Report. The sample Chart of Accounts (page 18) and sample Treasurer's Cash Report (pages 25-28) are designed to ease completion of Table 2.

The most recently updated copy of the Table 2 worksheet and Table 3 can be found by going to **www.gcfa.org** or contacting your district superintendent.

The Last Word, Sort Of

For many years the cartoon character Porky Pig, with the unforgettable voice of Mel Blanc, closed film cartoons with the trademark ending, "That's all folks." The folks who have put together this basic model for record keeping know it's not all there is, but they also know it will help get the job done.

You are encouraged to consider the more comprehensive approach to record keeping described in the appendix "The General Ledger Approach."

We also invite you to submit comments and suggestions on this handbook and forms for consideration when the next edition is printed. Please send your comments or suggestions to:

General Council on Finance and Administration
1 Music Circle North,
POB 340029
Nashville, TN, 37203-0029
email: gcfa@gcfa.org

May We Hear From You?

Your feedback will help us improve the Handbook. Please photocopy this page, complete the ratings, and mail it to GCFA at the address above. If you need more space, please attach additional sheets or examples. *Thanks!*

Please rate the following sections:

Work of the Counting Committee (pp. 5–12)
❑ Not Helpful   ❑ Helpful   ❑ Very Helpful
What changes would make this more useful to you?

_____
_____

Work of the Financial Secretary (pp. 12–16)
❑ Not Helpful   ❑ Helpful   ❑ Very Helpful
What changes would make this more useful to you?

_____
_____

Work of the Treasurer (pp. 17–33)
❑ Not Helpful   ❑ Helpful   ❑ Very Helpful
What changes would make this more useful to you?

_____
_____
_____

Appendix: The General Ledger Approach (pp. 35-68)
❑ Not Helpful   ❑ Helpful   ❑ Very Helpful
What changes would make this more useful to you?

_____
_____

Resources (page 69)
❑ Not Helpful   ❑ Helpful   ❑ Very Helpful
What changes would make this more useful to you?

_____
_____
_____

Illustrations and examples were:
❑ Not Helpful   ❑ Helpful   ❑ Very Helpful
What changes would make these more useful to you?

_____
_____
_____

Reproducible forms were:
❑ Not Helpful   ❑ Helpful   ❑ Very Helpful
Comments/suggestions: _____
_____
_____
_____

Church _____
City & State _____
—

Membership:
❑ up to 150   ❑ 151-500   ❑ over 500
If we may contact you, please provide your name and daytime phone number and/or email address.

_____
_____
_____

Appendix
The General Ledger Approach—
The Bridge to Financial Record Keeping on Computer

Introduction

Those familiar with bookkeeping and financial statements will have noticed that the basic record-keeping approach described in the body of this handbook has no STATEMENT OF FINANCIAL POSITION or standard STATEMENT OF ACTIVITIES. It also has no GENERAL LEDGER. The Treasurer's Report serves as both an abbreviated GENERAL LEDGER and the principal financial report.

Many churches, especially those with significant equipment, property, deferred gifts, or growing numbers of designated funds, may find that they need a more comprehensive record-keeping system, one that will provide direct conversion to a computerized system sometime in the future.

This appendix provides a complete manual record-keeping model that you can convert to a personal computer accounting system. If you are contemplating a computerized bookkeeping system, you must start with the concept of the GENERAL LEDGER.

A Note on Cash Accounting

There is some confusion among treasurers and pastors about cash accounting, which is used by most churches, districts, and conferences. Cash accounting does not do away with assets, liabilities, fund balances, balance sheets, or the GENERAL LEDGER. It merely means that you do not recognize income until it is received, whether in cash or property, and you do not recognize expenses until the bill is paid. You can still be on a cash accounting system even if you have a receivable such as a land contract for sale of the old parsonage and/or a payable such as the loan to pay for paving the parking lot.

Because nearly every church has some asset or liability that cannot be recorded in the checkbook, something more than the checkbook is needed to keep track of the finances of the church.

The Chart of Accounts and The General Ledger

You have heard the phrases, "keep the books," or "the company books," or "the books of accounts." All of these refer to the oldest and most basic bookkeeping document: The account ledger. The basic manual financial record-keeping model has a ledger page for each account and the collection of all these account pages is called the GENERAL LEDGER." You can still purchase ledger pages, and the heavy covers to keep them in, however for this modified approach, we have provided reproducible masters of the pages you need at the end of this section.

Chart of Accounts

The CHART OF ACCOUNTS is nothing more than a list of each account page in the general ledger book. For a computer, it becomes the "index" of accounts that the computer is tracking. You can start with any CHART OF ACCOUNTS and add or delete accounts as needed. The CHART OF ACCOUNTS provided on page 36 includes the categories of ASSETS and LIABILITIES AND FUNDS. In order to assist you at year-end, the expense portion of this chart follows the same basic order as the lines of the LOCAL CHURCH REPORT TO THE ANNUAL CONFERENCE, TABLE 1, FINANCIAL REPORT and TABLE 3, INCOME REPORT.

One group of accounts that you must identify for yourself is your list of the special and designated funds that your church has created. Give each fund a title and a number following the sequence of LIABILITIES on the CHART OF ACCOUNTS (accounts 251-289). Special and designated funds represent "liabilities" in the sense that they are funds that you have agreed to hold and use for a specific purpose. They are not part of the general operating funds of the church; therefore, they should not be treated as "income" or

CHART OF ACCOUNTS

Code # Account Title

ASSETS
120	Petty cash
121	Checking Account
122	Savings Account
123	Investments
125	Receivables
150	Equipment
151	Vehicles
152	Parsonage
154	Church
155	Land

LIABILITIES AND FUNDS
LIABILITIES
211	Payables
212	Social Security Tax Withholding
213	Federal Income Tax Withholding
214	State Income Tax Withholding
215	Local Income Tax Withholding
216	Group Insurance Withholding
217	Other Withholding
218	Employee/Pastor Withholding Reserves/Pension Withholding
219	Medicare Tax Withholding
220	Notes Payable
221	Long-Term Debt

FUNDS
250	Designated Benevolences
251-289	Designated & Special Funds
290	General Fund

INCOME
RECEIPTS FOR ANNUAL OPERATING BUDGET & BENEVOLENCE GIVING SOURCES
321	Received Through Pledges
325	Received from Non-pledging, yet Identified Givers
331	Received from Unidentified Givers
335	Received from Interest and Dividends
341	Received from Sale of Church Assets
345	Received through Building Use Fees, Contributions, Rentals
351	Received through Fundraisers and Other Sources

TOTAL ANNUAL OPERATING BUDGET & BENEVOLENCE RECEIPTS

RECEIPTS FOR CAPITAL AND OTHER SPECIAL PROJECTS
361	Capital Campaigns
365	Memorial/Endowment Bequests
371	Human Relations Day

Code # Account Title

372	One Great Hour of Sharing
373	Peace with Justice Sunday
374	Native American Ministries Sunday
375	World Communion
376	U.M. Student Day
391	Other Sources and Projects

TOTAL RECEIPTS CAPITAL AND OTHER SPECIAL PROJECTS

RECEIPTS FROM DISTRICT(S), ANNUAL CONFERENCE(S), JURISDICTIONAL CONFERENCE(S), GENERAL CHURCH AND/OR OTHER INSTITUTIONAL SOURCES OUTSIDE THE LOCAL CHURCH
| 381 | Equitable Compensation Funds Received by Church or Pastor |
| 385 | Advance Special or Apportioned Funds Received by Church |

TOTAL DISTRICT(S), ANNUAL CONFERENCE(S), JURISDICTIONAL CONFERENCE(S), GENERAL CHURCH AND/OR OTHER INSTITUTIONAL SOURCES OUTSIDE THE LOCAL CHURCH RECEIPTS

EXPENSES
BENEVOLENCES
401	World Service
402	Conference Benevolences
403	Ministerial Education Fund
404	Black College Fund
405	Africa University Fund
406	General Advance Specials
407	World Service Special Gifts
408	Youth Service Fund
409	Human Relations Day
410	One Great Hour of Sharing
411	Peace With Justice Sunday
412	Native American Ministries Sunday
413	World Communion
414	U.M. Student Day
415	Christian Education Sunday
416	Golden Cross Sunday
417	Rural Life Sunday
418	Disability Awareness Sunday
419	Conference Advance Specials
420	Other Conference Appeals
421	Higher Education
422	Health & Welfare Agencies
423	Other Benevolences Sent to Conference
424	Other Benevolences Paid Direct

CONNECTIONAL ADMINISTRATION FUNDS
441	Interdenominational Cooperation Funds
442	General Administration Fund
443	Jurisdictional Administration Fund
444	Area & Conference Administra-

Code # Account Title

| | tion Fund |
| 445 | District Administration Fund |

CONNECTIONAL CLERGY SUPPORT
461	Pension CRSP/CPP
462	Pension: Paid to Conference
463	District Superintendents' Fund
464	Episcopal Fund
465	Equitable Compensation Fund

LOCAL CHURCH CLERGY SUPPORT
501	Base Compensation: Pastor
502	Base Compensation: Associate
503	Housing & Utilities: Pastor
504	Housing & Utilities: Associate
507	Accountable Reimbursements: Pastor
508	Accountable Reimbursements: Associate
509	Other Cash Allowances: Pastor
510	Other Cash Allowances: Associate
511	Base Compensation: Deacon(s)
512	Housing & Utilities: Deacon(s)
513	Accountable Reimbursements: Deacon(s)
514	Other Cash Allowances: Deacon(s)

LOCAL CHURCH EXPENSES
521	Diaconal Minister/Deacon Salaries
522	Diaconal Minister/Deacon Fringe Benefits/Expenses
523	Other Staff Salaries
524	Other Staff Fringe Benefits/Expenses
525	Nurture & Membership
526	Church & Society
527	Church Education
528	Evangelism
529	Missions
530	Stewardship
532	Worship
533-538	Program Expenses
539	Other Program Expenses
540	Finance Committee
541	Office Expense
542	Repairs & Maintenance
543	Insurance
544	Church Utilities
545-548	Operating Expenses
549	Other Operating Expense
550	Interest Paid on Debt
551	Capital Improvements

"expense" to the church. When you receive funds for them, you add those funds directly to the balance sheet account; and when they are expended for their approved purpose, you subtract them directly from the balance sheet account.

The numbering of the accounts in the CHART OF ACCOUNTS is your privilege. The three-digit system provided is used by both small and medium-sized organizations. You may already have a CHART OF ACCOUNTS with a numbering system. If so, examine it carefully and adjust it as needed. Insert your own numbers, change the titles of accounts, and add any accounts that are needed for your particular church. The important thing is to adopt (or adapt) some numbering system for your CHART OF ACCOUNTS so that each transaction has general ledger code numbers for the positive (debit) and negative (credit) entries. Use of only account titles is subject to misinterpretation and sometimes they cannot be read years later.

A Home for Every Transaction

The CHART OF ACCOUNTS should provide a "home" for every single transaction that ever comes up in your church. If something new and different occurs, create a new account so that you can record it. That way nothing gets left in the bottom drawer because you didn't have a place to put it on the books.

General Ledger

The general ledger model provided in this appendix is organized with the accounts in columns so that you do not need a separate page for every account. All the sheets will fit into a standard notebook. Reproducible masters are provided for each type of ledger sheet you need. (Reproducible masters follow page 54.)

ASSETS—Two repro masters are provided for ASSETS. The first page includes standard accounts that most churches need; the second page has blank columns for your particular accounts.

LIABILITIES & FUNDS—Two repro masters are provided for LIABILITIES AND FUNDS. Again, the first page includes the standard accounts and the second page has blank columns for your particular accounts. It is here that you should list each of your designated funds so that you will have an exact track of the status of each category of designated gift or special fund created by the church and its donors.

INCOME—Two repro masters are provided for INCOME: One with standard accounts, one with blank columns.

EXPENSE—Two repro masters are provided for EXPENSE with standard accounts and blank columns for you to enter the expense accounts for your church.

Source Data and Documents

The financial data that goes into the GENERAL LEDGER comes from a variety of sources, most of which have special documents from which the data is collected during each month. These sources and their documents are:

(1) **Beginning Balances**: Taken from the existing set of "books" and various valuations by trustees, staff, and outside agencies;

(2) **Deposited Income**: Recorded in the CASH RECEIPTS JOURNAL;

(3) **Expenses**: Recorded in your checkbook and summarized in the CASH DISBURSEMENTS SUMMARY;

(4) **Payroll Expense and Liabilities**: Recorded in PAYROLL and PASTOR COMPENSATION SPREADSHEETS;

(5) **Non-Checkbook Income and Expense**: Recorded in JOURNAL ENTRY LEDGER;

(6) **Changes in Assets and Liabilities**: Recorded in JOURNAL ENTRY LEDGER;

(7) **Correction of Errors**: Recorded in JOURNAL ENTRY LEDGER.

Every financial event that occurs in the life of the church must have a place to be recorded in one of the listed sources. When all else fails, make a JOURNAL ENTRY so that the event does not get lost.

Reproducible masters of two of these documents are provided.

Initial Setup

In order to set up your new GENERAL LEDGER, you must assemble the beginning dollar values of each account that you intend to activate. If you start at the very beginning of a year it will be slightly simpler than starting during the year, since the beginning balances for all income and expense accounts will be "zero."

Consider the example shown below. Only a limited number of accounts are activated. You will notice that some balances are listed as positive numbers and some have parentheses, ( ), around them, which is a way to indicate a negative number. For ASSETS and LIABILITIES this is logical. ASSETS are what you own, therefore they should be positive; LIABILITIES are what you owe, therefore they should be negative. If ASSETS exceed LIABILITIES you have a positive NET WORTH; if Liabilities exceed Assets you have a negative NET WORTH.

General Fund Account Balance

To balance the books we must insert a number that offsets the NET WORTH and this number is called the GENERAL FUND. In the preceding example, ASSETS total $7,823.34, while LIABILITIES, including FUNDS, total $6,944.80. Therefore ASSETS exceed LIABILITIES by $878.54. If this was the beginning of the year we would insert (878.54) as the BEGINNING BALANCE for the GENERAL FUND. Then the negative numbers for LIABILITIES would add up to exactly the same total as

CASH DISBURSEMENT SUMMARY
JOURNAL ENTRY LEDGER

Account Number & Name		Beginning Balance	Source
ASSETS			
121	Checking	1023.34	Bank Statement
123	Investment	5000.00	C.D.
150	Equipment	800.00	Typewriter, Staff Estimate
151	Vehicles	1000.00	Tractor, Trustee Estimate
LIABILITIES AND FUNDS			
212	F.I.C.A.	(15.00)	Records in Drawer
213	Fed. Inc. Tax	(26.00)	Records in Drawer
214	State Inc. Tax	(10.00)	Records in Drawer
218	Emp. Reserves	(52.00)	Records in Drawer
220	Note Payable	(502.30)	Loan Payment, Call to Bank
251	Building Fund	(5000.00)	Records in Drawer
254	Memorial Fund	(1339.50)	Previous Books
290	General Fund	_____	*Leave blank for now*

INCOME
Total Annual Budget & Benevolence & Giving Funding Sources
        (755.30)   Year to Date from Books
Total Funding Sources for Capital and Other Special Projects
        (173.37)   Year to Date from Books
Total Funding Sources from District(s), Annual conference(s), Jurisdictional Conference(s), General Church and/or other institutional sources outside the local church
        (XXX.xx)   Year to Date from Books

EXPENSE			
406	General Advance	100.00	Year to Date from Books
461	MPP/CPP	60.00	Year to Date from Books
501	Pastor Comp.	400.00	Year to Date from Books
523	Oth. Staff Sal.	200.00	Year to Date from Books
544	Ch. Utilities	79.20	Year to Date from Books

Initial Setup Example
To balance the books, you must determine the balance for the GENERAL FUND ACCOUNT. See explanation above.

the positive numbers for ASSETS. When this occurs we say that the "books are balanced."

However, we have chosen to start this setup in the middle of the year; therefore, we must account for the fact that we have received income and disbursed funds since the first of the year. In order to make the books balance throughout the year a <u>convention</u> has been adopted for recording INCOME and EXPENSE. This accounting convention says that INCOME is recorded as a negative number and EXPENSE is recorded as a positive number. This convention is not logical—in fact it is counter intuitive—but it does work to keep the books balanced.

In the example, INCOME totals $928.67 and EXPENSE totals $839.20. Therefore INCOME is greater than EXPENSE by $89.47. Since INCOME is negative and is greater than the positive EXPENSE total, this difference must be ($89.47). Therefore, the GENERAL FUND balance at this time of the year is not really the ($878.54) that we thought it was. It has two pieces, ($89.47) from this year so far and ($789.07), which is the cumulation from all prior years. ($789.07 = $878.54 - $89.47) If we now go back and insert ($789.07) as the GENERAL FUND balance you will find that all the positive numbers, ASSETS of $7,823.34 and EXPENSE of $839.20, add up to $8,662.54; and, all the negative numbers, LIABILITIES of $6,944.80, INCOME of $928.67, and GENERAL FUND of $789.07, also add up to $8,662.54. Since the positive number total exactly equals the negative number total, the "books are balanced."

This action of adding up all the balances in all the accounts to see that the grand total is still zero is called "running the TRIAL BALANCE." You will use this exact technique at the end of every closing period, whether monthly or quarterly, and you will use it at year-end to close the books for one year and open them for the new year. These BEGINNING BALANCES should now be entered on the very top line of the appropriate pages of your GENERAL LEDGER so that the books are open, balanced, and ready for posting of transactions. (See below.)

Sample General Ledger   Church ___FIRST___   Year __2005__

Date	From	Checking Account 121	Investments 123	Equipment 150	Vehicles 151	F.I.C.A. 212	Federal Inc. Tax 213	State Inc. Tax 214	Emp/Pastor Reserves 218	Notes Payable 220	Designated Benevolence 250
3/1	BEG. BAL.	1023 34	5000 00	800 00	1000 00	(15 00)	(26 00)	(10 00)	(52 00)	(502 30)	— 0 —
3/31	CR3	489 65									(126 50)
3/31	CD3	(413 00)									126 50
3/31	PR3	(64 50)				(7 50)	(13 00)	(5 00)	(10 00)		
3/31	PC3	(184 00)							(16 00)		
3/31	JE 17	(10 00)									
3/31	JE 18		5000 00								
3/31	JE 19			80 00							
3/31	JE 20			(880 00)							
3/31	JE 21									502 30	
3/31	END BAL	841 49	10000 00	— 0 —	1000 00	(22 50)	(39 00)	(15 00)	(78 00)	— 0 —	— 0 —

SAMPLE GENERAL LEDGER   CHURCH FIRST   YEAR 2005

DATE	FROM	Building Fund 251	Memorial Fund 254	General Fund 290	REC'D FROM PLEDGERS 321	Non-Pledgers/ Identified Givers 325	General Advance 406	MPP/CPP 461	Pastor Compen. 501	Other Staff Salaries 523	Church Utilities 544
3/1	CR3	(5000 00)	(1339 50)	(789 07)	(255 30)	(173 37)	100 00	60 00	400 00	200 00	79 20
3/31	CD3	(60 00)	(23 85)		(238 00)	(41 30)					
3/31	PR3		220 00					28 00			38 50
3/31	PC3									100 00	
3/31	KE 17			10 00						200 00	
3/31	JE 18	(5000 00)									
3/31	JE 19			(80 00)							
3/31	JE 20			880 00							
3/31	JE 21			(502 30)							
3/31	END BAL	(10060 00)	(1133 35)	(491 37)	(993 30)	(214 67)	100 00	88 00	600 00	300 00	117 70

Data Collection and Monthly Posting

The most efficient approach to keeping the books is to post to the GENERAL LEDGER at the end of each month. For smaller churches, this posting could be done at the end of each quarter. Regardless of when the posting is made, the data must be collected almost daily on the source documents so that there is a something to post from.

Collecting Income Data

The methods of receiving offerings, pledges, and tithes are covered in the first section of this book. Use these methods regardless of which accounting system you choose. Reconcile each CASH RECEIPTS VOUCHER with a bank deposit ticket (see page 17-19) and make an entry on the CASH RECEIPTS JOURNAL (see page 19). Enter the date of the deposit, the voucher number and the total amount of the deposit to the CHECKING ACCOUNT in the three left-most columns of the CASH RECEIPTS JOURNAL. Then enter the distribution of the income to the various accounts (PLEDGES AND TITHES, LOOSE PLATE OFFERING, etc.) using ( ) around the income entries. (Remember that your CHECKING ACCOUNT is an asset account and is therefore entered as a positive number while the income accounts (PLEDGES AND TITHES, LOOSE PLATE OFFERING, etc.) are entered as negative numbers because of the accounting convention required to balance the books.) See example below.

Designated gifts for specific BENEVOLENCES, for example, GENERAL ADVANCE SPECIALS, must be recorded in a separate account and paid out at month end according to donor instructions. If you keep a variety of such gifts, you may need to keep a sub-ledger to keep track of the individual amounts and to whom they should be paid at month end.

All designated gifts and pledges received for SPECIAL FUNDS should be distributed directly to those fund accounts and not to any INCOME account. If it takes more than one line to enter all the special accounts on the CASH RECEIPTS JOURNAL sheet, use as many lines as you need, then draw a line across the entire page to segregate that multiple-line posting from the next one.

Before you leave that entry, make sure the total of the income accounts and the other account postings exactly equals the amount of the deposit to the CHECKING ACCOUNT. **IMPORTANT:** *Do not use this form to record deposits to any account other than the checking account.* You will use the JOURNAL ENTRY form to record non-checking-account deposits.

At the end of the month or the quarter draw a line across the entire page and total each column. For the OTHER ACCOUNTS, run a total for each separate account number referenced in the posting and record it below the line. Add up the totals across the page and make sure that the total of all income accounts and other accounts equals the total of all deposits made to the CHECKING ACCOUNT, column 3. You now have the INCOME data summarized and balanced for posting to the GENERAL LEDGER.

Collecting Expense Data

Almost all of your EXPENSE disbursements are made from the CHECKING ACCOUNT; therefore, the use of a CASH DISBURSEMENTS JOURNAL is a duplication of effort. **You can use your checkbook itself as the Disbursements Journal if you will mark on each check stub the Chart of Accounts number for that disbursement.**

CASH RECEIPTS JOURNAL   CHURCH *First*   Date   3/31/05 Page 2   "D"

Date	Voucher number	Checking Acct. 121	Rec'd from Pledgers	Rec'd from Non-pledgers/ identified Givers	Rec'd from Unidentified Givers	Interest/ Dividend	Sale of Church Assets	Building Use Fees Contributions Rentals	Fundraisers Others	Other Accounts
3/10	10	590 00	(250 00)	(75 00)	(15 00)			(225 00)		#365 (25.00)
3/13	11	103 85	(60 50)		(12 35)					#250 (6.00) #251 (20.00)
3/20	12	98 30	(58 50)		(9 30)					#254 (5.00)
3/27	13	186 00	(62 00)		(10 50)					#250 (12.00) #251 (10.00)
										#250 (8.50)
Mar. end		978 15	(431 00)	(75 00)	(47 15)	0 00	0 00	(225 00)	0 00	#250 (93.50) #251 (20.00)
										#365 (25.00)
										#250 (120.00)
										#251 (50.00)

If the check covers more than one account, record the amount and code number for each segment of the check and make sure the different listings add up to the total value of the check. See examples of check stubs on page 41. Don't forget that payments made from SPECIAL FUNDS get charged directly to those fund accounts and not to any EXPENSE account. For payroll checks mark the stub, "See Payroll or Pastor Compensation SpreadSheet Number X."

At the end of the month draw a line across the check stub and mark it "End of Posting for Month Y." Then follow these steps to prepare the batch for posting to the GENERAL LEDGER:

(1) Go to the beginning check for this month's posting and run a total of all checks issued to the "End of Posting for Month Y" line.

(2) Run a total of all deposits recorded on the check stubs during that same period.

(3) Record any adjustments to the account made by the bank, or you, which are recorded on the check stubs during the period.

(4) Take the beginning balance on the check stub at the start of the posting period, add the deposits, subtract the checks, and add or subtract the adjustments to see if you come out with the same balance on the check stub at the "End of Posting for Month Y" line. If not, proof the transactions to find the error and correct the check stub affected.

(5) Add up the value of paychecks issued during the period and compare to the total of paychecks calculated on the PAYROLL and PASTOR COMPENSATION SPREADSHEETS for the same period. If the totals do not match, proof the checks against the spreadsheets and correct any errors.

(6) Subtract the total value of paychecks from the total of all checks issued, found in step 1.

(7) **Cash Disbursement Summary**: Start with the first check in the posting period and record the CHART OF ACCOUNTS code number and the amount on a CASH DISBURSEMENTS SUMMARY sheet as shown below. Proceed to the next check and repeat the process. When you come to an account number that has already been recorded, add the newest check value to the total already recorded for that account number. Repeat until all checks and their account distribution have been recorded, except the paychecks.

(8) Run a total of all the account totals on the CASH DISBURSEMENTS SUMMARY sheet and compare to the total value of checks from step 6, which excluded paychecks. If it matches, record that total on the bottom of the CASH DISBURSEMENTS SUMMARY. Proof totals are shown in the illustration below.

You now have the EXPENSE data summarized and balanced for posting to the GENERAL LEDGER.

Cash Disbursements Summary

Month/Year 3/2005

Church FIRST   Page 3

Check Numbers: 434 to 439

Account No.		Total		Account No.		Total	
254	Memorial Fund	220	00		Beg. Balance	1023	34
544	Utilities	38	50		Total Checks	-661	50
250	Designated Benev.	126	50		Total Deposits	489	65
461	Pension	28	00		Adjustments	-10	00
		413	00		Ending Balance	841	49
121	Checking	(413	00)				
	Total Checks	661	50				
	Payroll	248	50				
	Net Disbursements	413	00				

CHECK STUBS

END OF POSTING – FEB	1023	34
No. 434	(10	00)
	101	50
Date _3/8/05_		
To _Roger's_		
Altar Service – In		
Memoriam Total	1114	84
254 – 220.00 This Check	220	00
Balance	894	84

No. 435 3/13	103	85
Date _3/16/05_		
To _General Power_		
and Light		
Utility Bill Total	998	69
544 – 38.50 This Check	38	50
Balance	960	19

No. 436 3/20	98	30
3/27	186	00
Date _3/29/05_		
To _John Grazen_		
Pastor Comp.		
Total	1244	49
(See Pastor This Check	184	00
Sheet 3)		
Balance	1060	49

No. 437		
Date _3/29/05_		
To _Conference office_		
Pension and Total	1060	49
Advance Special		
250 – 46.50 This Check	74	50
461 – 28.00 Balance	985	99
74.50		

No. 438		
Date _3/29/05_		
To _Martha Jones_		
Wages		
Total	985	99
(See Payroll This Check	44	50
Sheet 3)		
Balance	921	49

No. 439		
Date _3/29/05_		
To _Brown Office Equip._		
Adding Machine Total	921	49
Donated funds This Check	80	00
250 – 80.00 Balance	841	49

Collecting Payroll Data

The PAYROLL SPREADSHEETS, described on pages 30-31, are the basis for posting data to the GENERAL LEDGER. If the total of all paychecks as calculated on these sheets matches with the value of checks issued through the checking account (step 6 under "Collecting Expense Data," p. 52) then the TOTAL column on the sheet is the exact data that you will post to the GENERAL LEDGER.

If you have not proofed the TOTAL column to the detail lines and columns on each PAYROLL SPREAD-SHEET, you must do that and correct any errors before you begin posting the totals to the GENERAL LEDGER. Study the filled out example of a PAYROLL SPREADSHEET shown below.

All Other Transactions: the Journal Entry

If the financial transaction does not fall into the category of CHECKING ACCOUNT INCOME, CHECKING ACCOUNT EXPENSE, or PAYROLL, then it must become a JOURNAL ENTRY. The JOURNAL ENTRY is the most powerful bookkeeping tool there is. With it, *any* type of transaction can be recorded, no matter how exotic, and *any* mistake can be corrected. It is the treasurer's power over the books and makes the treasurer in command of the books instead of the books in command of the treasurer.

Keep each JOURNAL ENTRY transaction separate on the JOURNAL ENTRY LEDGER sheet so that you can spell out the reason for each transaction for future review or audit. Number the JOURNAL ENTRIES from the beginning of the year and keep all supporting data in an envelope or folder with the JOURNAL ENTRY number marked clearly on the supporting document(s).

JOURNAL ENTRIES are generally used for the following categories of transactions that churches experience:

(1) Donor-restricted gifts;
(2) Cash-in, cash-out transactions;
(3) Asset purchases, disposals, and transfers;
(4) Interest income and bank account adjustments;
(5) Non-cash transactions;
(6) Correcting mistakes.

Following are descriptions of each of these types of entries with examples shown on the JOURNAL ENTRY LEDGER page pictured on page 45.

Payroll Spread Sheet

Month/Year __3/05__   Church __FIRST__   Page __3__   Payroll Number __3__

Distribution \ Name	JOHN SMITH		MARTHA JONES		GEORGE BROWN								Total		
Gross Comp.	150	00	157	00	55	00							362	00	523
Excludable Fringe															
Group Insurance	(25	00)	—		—								(25	00)	216
Medical	(10	00)	(15	00)	—								(25	00)	218
Dependent Care	—		(40	00)	—								(40	00)	218
Life Insurance	—		—		—								—		
Pension	(5	00)	—		—								(5	00)	218
Reportable Comp.	110	00	102	00	55	00							267	00	TO 941
With/Deduction															
Social Security Tax	(6	82)	(6	32)	(3	41)							(16	55)	212
Medicare Tax	(1	60)	(1	48)		(80)							(3	88)	219
Fed. Inc. Tax	(4	00)	(2	00)	—								(6	00)	213
State Inc. Tax	(3	30)	(3	06)	(1	65)							(8	01)	214
Local Inc. Tax	(1	10)	(1	02)		(55)							(2	67)	215
Other Deductions															
CREDIT UNION	(5	00)	—		—								(5	00)	217
Net Compensation (Paycheck)	88	18	88	12	48	59							224	89	150

43

1. **Donor-restricted gifts:** If a donor gives money, securities, or property to the church that does not go directly into the checking account, then a JOURNAL ENTRY must be made. For example, Mr. Black may turn over a $5,000 certificate of deposit for the building fund that will mature in two years. It cannot be cashed in without a penalty, therefore it becomes an asset without being deposited. The coding is straightforward—it is an additional asset that increases the building fund, therefore:

+5,000 to 123 Investments   JE 18
(5,000) to 251 Building Fund

Similarly, Mrs. Brown may turn over a $1,000 savings account in memory of her husband. If the account is cashed in and deposited immediately to the church's savings account, then the coding is:

+1,000 to 122 Savings   JE 10
(1,000) to 254 Memorial Fund

2. **Cash-in, cash-out events:** The workcamp bus is ready to pull out of the parking lot, and Mr. Smith drives up, goes to the driver and hands him $100.00 to help with trip expenses. This is a valid contribution to the church and for a regularly budgeted project. It just didn't go through the checking account. You account for it by a JOURNAL ENTRY coded as follows:

(100.00) to 326 Youth Projects Income   JE 11
+100.00 to 539 Other Programs Expense

Similarly, if the missions chairperson holds out $15.00 from the proceeds of the cake sale for World Hunger to pay for the printing and tablecloths, you should make a JOURNAL ENTRY to recognize both the INCOME that wasn't deposited and the actual EXPENSE, coded as follows:

(15.00) to 325 Adult Projects Income   JE 12
+15.00 to 529 Missions Expense

3. **Asset purchases, disposals, and transfers:** Whenever ASSETS are purchased they need to be recognized as additions to the worth of the church even if they are purchased from operating funds. For example, if an add-on to the typewriter were

purchased with donated funds, the CASH DISBURSEMENTS SUMMARY would show:

(80.00) to 121 Checking Account
+80.00 to 250 Designated Benevolence

Nowhere is the value of the new asset recognized. Therefore a JOURNAL ENTRY is in order, coded as follows:

+80.00 to 150 Equipment Assets   JE 19
(80.00) to 290 General Fund Balance

Similarly, if the typewriter were stolen, an ASSET has been lost and the NET WORTH of the church is decreased. The JOURNAL ENTRY would be:

(880.00) to 150 Equipment Assets   JE 20
+880.00 to 290 General Fund Balance

If an ASSET is converted from one category to another, a JOURNAL ENTRY must be made. For example, a $3,000 savings account is collapsed and converted to a certificate of deposit. The coding would be:

(3,000) to 122 Savings Account   JE 13
+3,000 to 154 Investments Account

4. **Interest income and bank account adjustments:** All interest income requires a JOURNAL ENTRY; usually one per month should suffice. For example, last month the bank advised that the checking account has earned $12.39 in interest, the savings account $43.29, and a C.D. matured with interest paid of $66.00. The JOURNAL ENTRY should be:

+12.39 to 121 Checking Account   JE 14
+43.29 to 122 Savings Account
+66.00 to 123 Investments Account
(121.68) to 390 Miscellaneous Income

Similarly, for any bank adjustments, such as the charge for a certified check for a memorial plaque, a JOURNAL ENTRY must be made:

(10.00) to 121 Checking Account   JE 17
+10.00 to 254 Memorial Fund

Journal Entry Ledger

Church _____FIRST_____

Year _____

Page No. _3_

Date	#	Reason & Reference	Account Number	Debit "+" Amount	Credit "()" Amount	Posted to GL
2/5	10	Sarah Brown Savings Acct	122	1000.00		2/28
		to Memorial Fund	254		(1000.00)	"
2/14	11	Workcamp donation by	326		(100.00)	"
		Joe Smith	539	100.00		"
2/21	12	Cake sale expenses	325		(15.00)	"
		taken from proceeds	529	15.00		"
2/24	13	Transfer savings to	122		(3000.00)	"
		CD #1278693	123	3000.00		"
2/28	14	Interest Citizens Bank Chkg.	121	12.39		"
		Savgs.	122	43.29		"
		C.D.	154	66.00		"
		Income	390		(121.68)	"
2/28	15	McDonald estate settlement	155	10000.00		"
		Land for church	290		(10000.00)	"
2/28	16	Expense coding error	527		(85.00)	"
			532	85.00		"
3/2	17	Certified check for	121		(10.00)	3/31
		altar service	254	10.00		"
3/2	18	George Black CD for	121	5000.00		"
		Building Fund	251		(5000.00)	"
3/12	19	Capitalize add-on for	150	80.00		"
		typewriter	290		(80.00)	"
3/18	20	Typewriter stolen	150		(880.00)	"
			290	880.00		"
3/22	21	Cancelation of debt	220	502.30		"
			290		(502.30)	"

5. All non-cash transactions must use a Journal Entry to be recognized. For example, land is donated for general church use. The JOURNAL ENTRY would be:

+10,000.00 to 155 Land Assets   JE 15
(10,000.00) to 290 General Fund Balance

Similarly, the debt remaining for paving the parking lot is paid off by an anonymous donor. The bank advises that there is no remaining balance. The JOURNAL ENTRY recording the elimination of the debt would be:

+502.30 to 220 Note Payable   JE 22
(502.30) to 290 General Fund Balance

6. Correcting mistakes: For example, two months ago you paid a bill of $85.00 that was marked for Christian education expense. The Christian education chairperson was informed that she was over budget. When the expenses were reviewed it was found that the $85.00 should have been marked for worship expense. The JOURNAL ENTRY is as follows:

(85.00) to 527 Christian Education Expense   JE 16
+85.00 to 532 Worship Expense

You can also correct some mistakes that were made in prior years. For example, the audit committee finds that last year the payments made on the paving note were all expensed as interest. If you had not checked with the bank before setting up the books, the balance according to your records would have been $830.52. The auditors inform you that $328.22 should have been shown as reduction of principal, which would bring the balance down to the $530.02 that the bank reported to the auditors. The JOURNAL ENTRY that should be made for the prior months is:

+328.22 to 220 Notes Payable
(328.22) to 290 General Fund Balance because 328.22 extra expense was closed to the General Fund last year.

With all the applicable JOURNAL ENTRIES entered in the JOURNAL ENTRY LEDGER and an explanation sheet marked with the JOURNAL ENTRY number on it in a JOURNAL ENTRY file or envelope, you are ready to begin posting to the GENERAL LEDGER.

Posting the General Ledger
Gather your source documents:
—CASH RECEIPTS JOURNAL with the summary data for the month or quarter;
—CASH DISBURSEMENTS SUMMARY for the same period;
—PAYROLL SPREADSHEETS for that period; and
—JOURNAL ENTRY LEDGER pages for the period.

For every item you post to the GENERAL LEDGER, create an audit trail by identifying the source document in the column headed "FROM "

Use the following codes to designate the source document. The "x" represents the number of the month, quarter, payroll period, or JOURNAL ENTRY. For example, the posting reference "CR3" would be the CASH RECEIPTS JOURNAL sheet for <u>March</u>; "CR10" would be the sheet for <u>October</u>; "PR 6" would be the PAYROLL SPREADSHEET for the <u>sixth pay period</u>; etc. Smaller organizations may prefer to number source documents by the quarter rather than by the month.

Posting Reference Codes:

CASH RECEIPTS JOURNAL	=	CRx
CASH DISBURSEMENTS SUMMARY	=	CDx
PAYROLL SPREADSHEET	=	PRx
JOURNAL ENTRY LEDGER	=	JEx

Start Posting from Cash Receipts Journal

Start from the CASH RECEIPTS JOURNAL sheets. On the line immediately below the last line of balances entered on the general ledger pages, enter the date in the DATE column and the posting reference code in the FROM column. The posting reference code for the CASH RECEIPTS JOURNAL sheet is CRx with "x" as the appropriate month or quarter. (See the sample shown on page 40.) Then begin to post the figures from the summary line you prepared on the CASH RECEIPTS JOURNAL. Start with the CHECKING ACCOUNT total and proceed with all the applicable INCOME, SPECIAL FUND, or other accounts. You may wish to add the entries on the line to make sure they total zero; however, since you did that in preparing the data to start with, you may choose not to bother with this unless an error is indicated.

The Most Common Errors in Posting
(1) Transposition of numbers, e.g., reading 802.00 and writing 820.00
(2) Omitting an entry.
(3) Entering a negative number (credit) as positive.

Post from the Cash Disbursements Sheet

Next post from the CASH DISBURSEMENTS SUMMARY sheet. Enter the posting date and the posting reference code (CDx, with "x" being the appropriate month or quarter), then begin to post the figures that you prepared and proofed on the CASH DISBURSEMENTS SUMMARY, starting with the CHECKING ACCOUNT total and proceeding with all the applicable EXPENSE, SPECIAL FUND, and other accounts. Again, you may wish to add the entries on this line to make sure they total zero; or wait to see if there may be an error.

Post from the Payroll Spreadsheets

Next post from the PAYROLL SPREADSHEETS. Enter the posting date and code (PRx with "x" being the appropriate pay period) for the first PAYROLL SPREADSHEET. Post the CHECKING ACCOUNT total (i.e. NET COMPENSATION or PAYCHECK) from the bottom of the spreadsheet and then proceed to enter the other figures in the appropriate LIABILITY and EXPENSE accounts. Proceed to the next applicable PAYROLL SPREADSHEET and repeat until each PAYROLL SPREADSHEET has been posted to a line on the GENERAL LEDGER.

Post from Journal Entry Ledger

Last, post from the JOURNAL ENTRY LEDGER sheets. Enter the posting date and code (JEx with "x" being the appropriate journal entry item number). Since JOURNAL ENTRIES are usually scattered among the accounts in the GENERAL LEDGER, you have two choices in posting them:

(1) Post each JOURNAL ENTRY on a separate line as shown on page 39.
(2) Post all of them on a single line but mark the applicable JOURNAL ENTRY number alongside each entry. (You can do this only with a manual system. A computer may require a separate or "split" entry.)

Closing the Books

When you have finished posting all the data for the month or quarter, you are ready to close the books for that period. Draw a line across all the pages of the GENERAL LEDGER and retotal each column, adding to or subtracting from the BEGINNING BALANCE, as appropriate, and entering the new BALANCE for each column under the line. For those columns with no transactions for the month, or quarter, bring down the previous BALANCE, even if it is zero. Remember, if the BEGINNING BALANCE is positive and the transaction is positive the new BALANCE will be simply the total of the two. If the BEGINNING BALANCE is negative and the transaction is also negative then the new BALANCE will be even more negative, again the total of the two but with ( ) around it. Be careful when the transactions are the opposite sign from the usual BALANCE. This is the third most common source of error in bookkeeping.

Trial Balance

After you have recalculated the BALANCE for each column you then must run a new TRIAL BALANCE. On an adding machine, preferably with a tape, enter each BALANCE from across each page, entering the positive ones with the "+" key and the negative ones with the "-" key, starting with the ASSETS and proceeding to the end of EXPENSES, preferably in CHART OF ACCOUNTS order. When you finish, press the total key and pray that the total is "zero." If it is, you have balanced and closed the books for that period.

If the TRIAL BALANCE is not zero, you must retrace your steps in the following order until you find the error:

(1) Examine the adding-machine tape and check every number on the tape against the number in the column it came from. You may find you put a wrong number in the adding machine.

(2) Check the columns with no transactions to make sure you brought down the same number for the BALANCE that was there before.

(3) Recalculate the BALANCES for those columns with odd transactions, e.g., "positive" transactions in "negative" columns.

(4) Recalculate all other columns for ending BALANCES.

(5) Retotal each posting line to make sure it adds up to zero.

(6) Run a new TRIAL BALANCE on the BEGINNING BALANCES to make sure you didn't have an error built in from the last time.

(7) Go back to step 1 and search again.

When you reach the end of your rope and still haven't found the error, consider how big the mistake is. If it is only a few pennies or a dollar, "plug it" in either MISCELLANEOUS INCOME or MISCELLANEOUS EXPENSE, depending on whether you need more "negative" to balance (= INCOME) or more "positive" (= EXPENSE). Enter it in an appropriate column with a circle around it and retotal that column including the "plug." You should then have a zero TRIAL BALANCE and you can let the audit committee try to find the mistake.

You are now ready to prepare the financial reports that are needed for your pastor, staff, finance committee, and church council.

Financial Reports

There are three basic reports that you can prepare from your GENERAL LEDGER:
—STATEMENT OF FINANCIAL POSITION
— STATEMENT OF ACTIVITIES
—SPECIAL FUNDS TRANSACTIONS

Statement of Financial Position

The STATEMENT OF FINANCIAL POSITION is the world's oldest and most reliable financial report. It is the only document that reveals the true financial worth and health of an organization. Very little can be hidden from the STATEMENT OF FINANCIAL POSITION as people who specialize in corporate mergers and acquisitions know very well. The more complete you make the STATEMENT OF FINANCIAL POSITION, the more accurately you will portray the organization's financial health.

The format for the STATEMENT OF FINANCIAL POSITION is up to your organization. A model format is provided with this book. However you construct it, you should make sure that *all* the ASSET and LIABILITY

AND FUNDS accounts are included. This is best done by taking the format and writing down on which line each account number goes from the CHART OF ACCOUNTS. The STATEMENT OF FINANCIAL POSITION does not contain *any* INCOME or EXPENSE accounts. The only recognition of the operating accounts is the line labeled "CURRENT SURPLUS/ (DEFICIT)." That number comes from the INCOME AND EXPENSE STATEMENT and is merely the total of all income year to date minus the total of all expense year to date. Since your GENERAL LEDGER is balanced according to the steps described above, the STATEMENT OF FINANCIAL POSITION should be balanced after you put all the totals in the right places. The sample STATEMENT OF FINANCIAL POSITION shown on the following page uses the data from the sample GENERAL LEDGER shown on page 38 and includes the identification of which accounts go onto which lines.

Statement of Activities

The STATEMENT OF ACTIVITIES is the same as the Profit and Loss Report in the business world. It can be very misleading to use in assessing the worth and health of an organization, including a church; however, if it is accurately maintained, it is an excellent way to monitor the operating management of the church.

Again the format of this report is up to you. A model format has been included with this book. However you construct it, you should make sure that *all* of the STATEMENT OF ACTIVITIES accounts are included. This can best be done by taking the format and writing down each account number from the CHART OF ACCOUNTS beside the line where it will be entered. The STATEMENT OF ACTIVITIES contains *only* INCOME and EXPENSE accounts. There is no provision for showing transactions on STATEMENT OF FINANCIAL POSITION accounts such as SPECIAL FUNDS or WITHHOLDING ACCOUNTS. These can be reported another way as shown in later paragraphs. The sample STATEMENT OF ACTIVITIES, on the page 50 uses the data from the sample GENERAL LEDGER shown on page 39 and, shows the designation of which line includes each account.

The model format also includes columns to track the comparison of the actual INCOME and EXPENSE data with the budgets established for the year and for the period.

Statement of Financial Position

Balance Sheet

Church _____ FIRST _____
Month/Year _____ March 2005 _____

ASSETS

Cash (121)	$	841.49
Investments (123)		10000.00
Receivables (125)		—
Property (150, 152)		1000.00
Other ( )		—

TOTAL ASSETS $ 11841.49

LIABILITIES & FUNDS

LIABILITIES

Payables (212, 213, 214, 218)	$	154.50
Debts (220)		—0—
Prepaid Income ( )		—
Other ( )		—

Sub-Total Liabilities 154.50

FUNDS

Donor Restricted (250, 251, 254)	11193.35
Church Restricted ( )	
Suspense Accounts ( )	
Other ( )	
General Fund (290)	491.37
Current Surplus/(Deficit)	2.27

Sub-Total Funds 11686.99

TOTAL LIABILITIES & FUNDS $ 11841.49

Statement of Activities

Church __FIRST__

Month/Year __March 2005__

	Month to Date	Year to Date	Budget to Date	Total Budget
INCOME				
Total Receipts from Annual Operating Budget & Benevolences Giving Funding Sources	338.90	1023.96		
Total Funding Sources for Capital and Other Special Projects	150.00	1200.00		
Total Funding Sources from Districts, Annual Conference, Jurisdictional Conf., Gen. Church and/or other institutional sources outside the local church	0.00	0.00		
TOTAL INCOME	488.90	2223.96		
EXPENSES				
Program areas (_____)				
Church Administration (__523__)	100.00	300.00		
Pastor & Support (__461, 501__)	228.00	688.00		
Facility & Maintenance (__542__)	38.50	117.70		
Apportionments (_____)				
Askings (_____)				
Advance Specials (__406__)	-0-	100.00		
Other Benevolences (_____)				
Miscellaneous (_____)				
TOTAL EXPENSES	366.50	1205.70		
CURRENT SURPLUS/(DEFICIT)	$ 121.80	1,018.26		

Special Fund Report

Account __254__ Fund __Memorial__ _____ Date __3/31/05__

		Deposits	Withdrawals
Balance 1/1/05	845.30		
Deposits — Jan through March		768.05	
Nursery Furniture			250.00
Altar Service			230.00
Balance 3/31/05	1133.35		

Special Funds Transactions

Since the STATEMENT OF FINANCIAL POSITION does not report transaction data and the STATEMENT OF ACTIVITIES does not include SPECIAL FUNDS, there may be times when one of the boards or the pastor needs to know the status of a SPECIAL FUND. The way in which this is done with a computer system is to ask for a printout of the GENERAL LEDGER account for a specific SPECIAL FUND. With the manual system you can do the same thing with a copier, but you may have to translate the shorthand description of your posting system. You may prefer to create a SPECIAL FUND REPORT in the format shown on page 51.

To prepare such a report, review each transaction posted to the GENERAL LEDGER for the year and provide a simple description of it. Sometimes repetitive transactions of the same type can be grouped together to streamline the presentation. Use your judgment on each such report to make it as meaningful as possible for those who need to use it.

Year-end Closing and Opening the New Year

At the end of the financial year, you will close the books exactly the same way as for any other month or quarter; and you should produce a set of financial reports for that last month, which will also be the year-end financial report. Your church may want a summary report for each SPECIAL FUND as a part of these year-end books. If you are using a computer system, you will want to print out the entire GENERAL LEDGER for the year as a permanent record.

You must accomplish some additional steps to prepare the books for the new financial year. It is usually recommended that a new set of GENERAL LEDGER pages be opened for the start of the new year. This provides an opportunity to drop some old account columns and to reorder some of the newer ones for easier posting. You will especially need a new set of INCOME and EXPENSE pages since *all* of these accounts start over with a BEGINNING BALANCE of "zero" for the new year.

The ASSET and LIABILITIES AND FUNDS pages need to be posted with the FINAL BALANCES from the old year as the BEGINNING BALANCES for the new year; *except for the GENERAL FUND BALANCE.* The GENERAL FUND BALANCE from the end of the previous year is adjusted by the year-end surplus or deficit from the previous year. This is the action that allows all the INCOME and EXPENSE accounts to start over at "zero." If the year-end INCOME exceeded year-end EXPENSE, i.e., a surplus, then the GENERAL FUND increases by that amount, i.e., it gets more negative. If the year-end EXPENSE was greater than the year-end INCOME, i.e., a deficit, then the GENERAL FUND BALANCE decreases, i.e., becomes less negative. If the books were closed out in our sample GENERAL LEDGER on page 39 the year- to-date surplus of 2.27 shown on page 49 would have been "closed to the General Fund" and the GENERAL FUND account, 290, would have been increased, i.e., more negative since the surplus is excess income, which is negative, from (491.37) to (493.64). This is not entered as a JOURNAL ENTRY but is a single transaction change in the opening balance of the GENERAL FUND. In a computer accounting system, this is accomplished automatically as the INCOME and EXPENSE account balances are "zeroed" for the beginning of the year.

After you have entered all the new BEGINNING BALANCES, including the adjusted GENERAL FUND BALANCE, you should run a new TRIAL BALANCE to make sure that the total of all BEGINNING BALANCES is still zero.

Computerization

A new treasurer or financial secretary may find a computerized record system already in place, or may want to change from a manual system to a computerized one. Churches that want to computerize all or part of their record-keeping systems will find a variety—sometimes a bewildering variety—of equipment and software to consider.

The software available will include:

—generic systems designed for churches

—general purpose accounting systems, which may, with varying degrees of difficulty, be adapted to church use

—multipurpose software, such as any of a number of spreadsheet, word processing, or database packages, which may lend themselves to one or more of the functions involved in local church financial record keeping.

Before you choose any computer equipment or software, do some investigating:

—Talk with your Conference Treasurer for current information and guidance regarding both hardware and software appropriate for a local church application. Conference Treasurers meet annually with hardware/software vendors and are a prime resource for you.

—Talk with the pastor, the church secretary, the membership secretary, and any other local church officers who may need to use a computer for the tasks they do in the church. Be sure that any new equipment will meet the needs of as many potential users in the life of the church as possible. Any purchase of software and hardware should be dictated by the needs of potential users.

—Talk with other church treasurers and financial secretaries about any experiences they have had with computerizing their work.

—Evaluate potential digital solutions through demonstration or trial software.

Software packages are available specifically for churches. They usually provide not only financial record-keeping modules, but membership and contribution modules as well. An advantage of a system with a membership module is that it is linked with the contributions module. This allows you to enter weekly contributions into the financial system and automatically update the accumulative contributions of individual contributors. You can more easily prepare quarterly, monthly, annual, or other periodic contributions statements for your contributors.

Computer System Installation

1. **Establish a complete Chart of Accounts.** If you haven't expanded your CHART OF ACCOUNTS to include ASSETS, LIABILITIES, and FUNDS accounts, you must do so before you can set up a computer record-keeping system. You must also establish a code number format that will be compatible with the computer software that you select.

2. **Carefully read and follow the directions** that come with your new church software package. Make use of the consulting feature you purchased with the software: Call for help. It will be easier to head off trouble later if you spend time to set up the system correctly at the beginning.

Reproducible Masters

Reproducible masters for the General Ledger Approach begin on the next page and include the following items:

—Cash Disbursement Summary sheet

—Payroll SpreadSheet

—Journal Entry Ledger sheet

—General Ledger ASSETS sheet
   with standard accounts column headings

—General Ledger ASSETS sheet
   with blank columns headings

—General Ledger LIABILITIES sheet
   with standard accounts column headings

—General Ledger LIABILITIES sheet
   with blank columns headings

—General Ledger INCOME sheet
   with standard accounts column headings

—General Ledger INCOME sheet
   with blank columns headings

—General Ledger EXPENSE sheet
   with standard accounts column headings

—General Ledger EXPENSE sheet
   with blank columns headings

—Statement of Financial Position

—Statement of Activities

—Special Fund Report

Cash Disbursements Summary

Month/Year _____

Church _____

Check Numbers: _____ to _____

Page _____

Account No.	Total

Account No.		Total

Payroll SpreadSheet

Month/Year _____

Church _____

Payroll Number _____

Name / Distribution						Total
Gross Comp.						
Excludable Fringe						
Group Insurance						
Medical						
Dependent Care						
Life Insurance						
Pension						
Reportable Comp.						
With/Deduction						
Social Security Tax						
Medicare Tax						
Fed. Inc. Tax						
State Inc. Tax						
Local Inc. Tax						
Other Deductions						
Net Compensation (Paycheck)						

Journal Entry Ledger

Church _____

Year _____

Date	#	Reason & Reference	Account Number	Debit "+" Amount	Credit "()" Amount	Posted to GL

General Ledger–Assets

Church _____ Year _____ Page A– _____

Date	From	Land	Church	Equipment	Parsonage	Furnishings	Vehicles	Checking Account	Petty Cash	Savings	Investments

General Ledger–Assets

Church ————————— Year ————— Page A–————

*Enter your own titles and/or chart of account numbers

Date	From																								

General Ledger–Liab/Funds   Church   Year ____ Page L–___

Date	From	Payables	Social Security	Medicare Tax	Federal Inc. Tax	State Inc. Tax	Local Inc. Tax	Group Insurance	Other Witholding	Emp/Pastor Reserves	Notes Payable

General Ledger–Liab/Funds   Church _____   Year _____   Page L–_____

*Enter your own titles and/or chart of account numbers

Date	From																											

61

General Ledger–Income

Church _____   Year _____   Page I– _____

Date	From	Through Pledges	Non-Pledging Identified	Unidentified Givers	Interest Dividend	Sale of Church Assets	Building Use, Fees	Fundraisers, Other	Capital Campaign	Other Amount

General Ledger–Income

Church _____

*Enter your own titles and/or chart of account numbers

Date	From																							

General Ledger–Expenses

Church _____ Year _____ Page E–____

Date	From	World Service	Ministerial Education	Black Col. Univ. Fund	Africa Univ. Fund	General Advance	World Serv. Spl.	Youth Service	Gen. Church Offerings	Conference Offerings	Conference Advance	Mission Initiatives

General Ledger–Expenses

Church _____ Year _____ Page E–___

* Enter your own titles and/or account numbers

Date	From												

Statement of Financial Position

Church _____

Month/Year _____

ASSETS

Cash (_____) $ _____

Investments (_____)   _____

Receivables (_____)   _____

Property (_____)   _____

Other (_____)   _____

                                                                              _____

TOTAL ASSETS $ _____

LIABILITIES & FUNDS

LIABILITIES

Payables (_____) $ _____

Debts(_____)   _____

Prepaid Income (_____)   _____

Other (_____)   _____

Sub-Total Liabilities   _____

FUNDS

Donor Restricted (_____

_____)   _____

Church Restricted (_____

_____)   _____

Suspense Accounts (_____

_____)   _____

Other (_____)   _____

General Fund (_____)   _____

Current Surplus/(Deficit)   _____

Sub-Total Funds   _____

                                                                              _____

TOTAL LIABILITIES & FUNDS $ _____

Statement of Activities

Church _____

Month/Year _____

	Month to Date	Year to Date	Budget to Date	Total Budget
INCOME				
Total Receipts from Annual Operating Budget & Benevolences Giving Funding Sources.............	_____	_____	_____	_____
Total Funding Sources for Capital and Other Special Projects.................................	_____	_____	_____	_____
Total Funding Sources from Districts, Annual Conference, Jurisdictional Conf., Gen. Church and/or other institutional sources outside the local church........	_____	_____	_____	_____
TOTAL INCOME	_____	_____	_____	_____
EXPENSES				
Program areas (_____)	_____	_____	_____	_____
Church Administration (_____)	_____	_____	_____	_____
Pastor & Support (_____)	_____	_____	_____	_____
Facility & Maintenance (_____)	_____	_____	_____	_____
Apportionments (_____)	_____	_____	_____	_____
Askings (_____)	_____	_____	_____	_____
Advance Specials (_____)	_____	_____	_____	_____
Other Benevolences (_____)	_____	_____	_____	_____
Miscellaneous (_____)	_____	_____	_____	_____
TOTAL EXPENSES	_____	_____	_____	_____
CURRENT SURPLUS/(DEFICIT) $	_____	_____	_____	_____

Special Fund Report

Account _____ Fund _____ Date _____

	Deposits	Withdrawals
Balance		

Resources

- GCFA.org (for charge conference forms, audit information, and much more)
- Cokesbury.com (to order Stewardship resources and supplies such as Offering Envelopes and the Quarterly Report of Giving)
- Christianity Today International (US) www.churchlawandtax.com

BOOKS

Not Your Parents' Offering Plate
A New Vision for Financial Stwardship
ISBN 13: 9781501804922. Abingdon Press
J. Clif Christopher knows what people think as they pass the offering plate. "We give to lots of charities—I don't need to donate to the church." Chances are, many who sit in your congregation think the same thing. Christopher, a former pastor, has consulted with hundreds of churches. In this book, he shows how to demonstrate the impact of financial gifts and offers realistic guidance on how to ask individuals to increase their giving. His instruction is a perfect read for pastors and stewardship teams.

The Church Money Manual
Best Practices for Finance and Stewardship
ISBN 13: 9781426796579. Abingdon Press
The church leader's guide to thoughtfully managing church finances. Each mini-chapter attacks a particular problem related to church money management and stewardship. Planned giving, finance committee member selection, and strategies to increase end-of-year giving are a few of the topics covered in this go-to resource for any size church.

STEWARDSHIP PROGRAMS

Enough Stewardship Program Guide
Discovering Joy through Simplicity and Generosity
Revised Edition with Flash Drive
ISBN 13: 9781501857928. Abingdon Press
Church Leaders are struggling to help their congregations respond to the sometimes dramatic ebb and flow of the economy. While their memers are simply trying to stay afloat financially, the budget of the church is suffering as well. In the midst of all of this, though, there is God and a divine calling for each of us. Adam Hamilton offers a simple campaign that will transform how the church and individuals review the role of money in connection with their life's purpose and the positive impact

that transformation will have on the world. This program is designed for church-wide and small-group studies and includes:
> A campaign timeline
> Sample communication pieces
> Sermon series notes
> Artwork for PowerPoint and signage

Transformed Giving, Realizing Your Church's Full Stewardship Potential, A Forty-day Stewardship Program for Churches of All Sizes, featuring *Treasures of the Transformed Life* by John Ed Mathison. *Program Kit* ISBN 9780687334353. Abingdon Press.

New Consecration Sunday Stewardship Program Manual, with guest leader guide & CD-ROM. ISBN 9780687644377. Abingdon Press. A simple and direct approach focused on the spiritual perspective.

Handbooks & Guidelines

2017-2020 UM Church Financial Records Handbook, ISBN 9781501835711.

Guidelines for Leading Your Congregation
Finance: Handling God's Money in the Church, ISBN 9781501829666.

Trustees: Manage the Resources of the Congregation, ISBN 9781501829994.

Stewardship: Raise Up Generous Disciples, ISBN 9781501829963.

Church Council: Connect Vision and Ministry in Your Church, ISBN 9781501830303.

Official Forms and Supplies

Developed for your financial programs by GCFA and approved by the Committee on Forms and Records for The United Methodist Church.

—**A Commitment to the Church (Pledge Card)**
978-0-687-43047-5
—**Quarterly Report of Giving** 978-0-687-43049-9
—**Quarterly Report of Giving, window envelope** 978-0-687-43050-5

Offering Envelopes

—**Bulk and custom offering envelopes**. Call to request a free catalog of offering envelope selections including bulk envelopes, numbered boxed sets, and Monthly Mailing programs. Offering envelopes encourage pledges and provide records for the church, stewardship reminders, a consistent method of giving, confidentiality, and convenience.